TEACHING TO WONDER

TEACHING TO WONDER

Spiritual Growth
Through Imagination
and Movement

Judy Gattis Smith

A Griggs Educational Resource
Published by
Abingdon Press/Nashville

TEACHING TO WONDER: SPIRITUAL
GROWTH THROUGH IMAGINATION AND MOVEMENT

Copyright © 1989 by Abingdon Press

This book is printed on acid-free paper.

Library of Congress Cataloging-in-Publication Data

Smith, Judy Gattis, 1933–
  Teaching to wonder.
  (A Griggs educational resource)
  Includes index.
  1. Christian education of children.
2. Imagination in children. 3. Movement education. I. Title.
BV1475.2.S635   1989   268'.432   88-34445

ISBN 0-687-41123-8 (alk. paper)

Scripture quotations are from the Good News Bible—Old Testament: Copyright © American Bible Society 1976; New Testament: Copyright © American Bible Society 1966, 1971, 1976.

The prayer on page 54 is from *Images of Peace* by Pat Corrick Hinton, p. 25, Winston Press, 1984.

The sample shields on page 71 are from *Symbols of the Church* copyright © 1959 by Carroll E. Whittemore. Used by permission of the publisher, Abingdon Press.

MANUFACTURED BY THE PARTHENON PRESS AT
NASHVILLE, TENNESSEE, UNITED STATES OF AMERICA

For my children,
Neel and Candace,
Sally and Steve

And my husband,
David

CONTENTS

Introduction   11

PART 1—Imagination/Fantasy   15

PART 2—Kinesthetics/Movement   39

PART 3—Word/Symbol   57

PART 4—Antithesis/Paradox   77

Outline of Experiences   93

John Wesley in his *Journal* for July 18, 1784, wrote: "I find [Sunday] schools springing up wherever I go. Perhaps God may have a deeper end therein than men are aware of. Who knows but some of these schools may become nurseries for Christians?"

INTRODUCTION

There is something that has always puzzled me. How can two children sit in a church school classroom experiencing the same lesson and one be moved to an awareness of God and the other remain unmoved, untouched, even bored? Or, how can the same lesson be taught to children of a similar age and one group become excited and motivated and the other remain unmoved? God's Spirit is always present. Is the Spirit more present to some than to others? Is it possible to learn more on this subject? Perhaps we can receive a hint from Hebrews 4:2: "For we have heard the Good News, just as they did. They heard the message, but it did them no good, because when they heard it, they did not accept it with faith."

The missing link seems to be faith development. The possibility of cultivating faith is present in the church school classroom. We can cultivate the faith that undergirds and explains the message.

Although skills and curricula content, techniques and methods, technology and social activism will continue to be a focus, they can be strengthened as we affirm our spiritual roots and follow the impulses and nudges that lead to action.

We can know God personally and intimately as well as learning about God. We can experience the life-giving power of the church school and the enriching of the personal lives of our students. As we attempt to tell and explain the faith, we keep before us these words of Scripture:

Find out for yourself how good the Lord is. Ps. 34:8

In the past I knew only what others had told me, but now I have seen you with my own eyes. Job 42:5

Faith is something that must be responded to individually. We can train. We can nurture. But ultimately it is the individual who responds. We report on personal experiences, not on reports of reports of reports. Personal experience is our only possible authority. Personal experience cannot be doubted.

How does this firsthand meeting with God take place? Is it possible in our church school? I think it is and I think being aware of this meeting is an exciting way to teach. It recognizes the fact that there is an insistent, imperative, glorious yearning for God in the human spirit. The teacher begins here. Study comes second, not first. First is worship and opening ourselves to God.

This calls for a distinctive kind of education and sensitizing to God's presence, a willingness to listen for God's word and to respond.

We can contrast it with computer education, which is becoming so dominant in public school teaching. Computers teach exactness, one answer, correctness. We teach intuition, feeling, sensitivity. Computers use logic and sequence. We search for meaning and purpose. Computers ask, How? We ask, Why? The result for computers is a printed page, a hard copy, an exact answer. The result for us is dedicated and committed lives.

In church school we must abandon the security of computer languages where everything says what it means and means what it says and where the problem is not one of understanding but one of communication, of relationship, of covenant.

The purpose of Christian education, it seems to me, is quite different from other forms of education that we know. It is designed to bring about the relationship between humans and God, which the church knows as faith. And we circle back to what we said in the beginning paragraph that faith development is the intimate, proximate, sensuous, personal teaching of the faith. What methods shall we use? How can our timeless treasures be presented to children? We have a wide range of choices. We turn to imagination, emotion, instincts. We teach subjectively and intuitively. We teach children to become clear and trusting in their own perceptions. We cultivate the capacity to wonder, and have freshness of insight. We emphasize the inner experience, the mystery of the divine presence in our lives. We help children discover a secret place, a fertile darkness in which tender things may take root and grow.

Our children need to ponder, to reflect, to contemplate, to work carefully through a subject, to be comfortable with silence. They need to dwell on noble thoughts, courage, compassion, generosity, and simple kindness. Children need to tune themselves to the mood of universal love, sharing, and experiencing peace and happiness. And they need to have fun doing it.

It is a multidimensional process. It is a potpourri of experiences.

It involves senses that operate independently of reason and logic. It involves the hunching skill. We learn from impressions, feelings, inclinations, and vibrations.

Our traditional evaluation tools will not be adequate for this type of learning and this may be frustrating for teachers. But how do you evaluate improved skills in wonder, how do you measure if learning has taken place in meaning and depth of life?

What Is This Book and Who Is It For?

To teach relationally, to cultivate a deeper involvement, we need different tools. We fumble and stumble when we try to imitate secular education. Factual knowledge, logic, and sequence will not help children discern God's person and will not teach the mystery whereby they will love God more dearly.

The senses (hearing, seeing, smelling, touching, and tasting) are wonderful avenues for getting in touch with God. A few years ago I wrote a book about using these senses in faith development. In response to this book, church school teachers shared with me other styles of learning. It was exciting for me to come to realize that sensory and intuitive learning involves more than the five traditional or classic senses. And so, this book seeks to teach about God through other sensory means.

Fellow church school teachers, this book is for you. You are the ones who provide a setting for learning, who look for the unusual meaning in the usual event, who encourage creative exploration. I have attempted to provide concrete experiences that you can try with your church school class. I hope my suggestions will only be starting points for you. As you become excited about this style of teaching you will think of more possibilities than I have ever tried. I share with you my ideas, which have been experienced with actual church groups with varying forms of success, and I strongly encourage you to create with your class your own experiences. Experienced teachers will have their own methods and of course will cull only what they need. Less experienced ones may be interested in some of the ways these exercises were used. Go deep within yourself and trust your perceptions. You and your class can develop the personal ability to experience the sacred.

Classroom Climate

In this type of learning, the climate of our classroom is especially important.

First, there should be wonder in a classroom engaged in this kind of learning. Wonder that is astonishment at God's power and activity.

Pause and examine the breathtaking beauty of a butterfly's wing. Feel the fabric of a feather. Examine the intricate structure of a snowflake. Look at the exquisite symmetry of a seashell. Wonder and contemplate. The relatedness of things of the natural world invests life with a depth, a presence, a value.

A sense of wonder at God's creation inspires us with a desire to understand and know the Creator more fully. Wonder keeps us growing and learning in faith.

One of the important benefits of working with children is the chance it gives adults to recapture the miraculous sense of wonder. In this area we are not always the wise ones. Watching a child learn is inspiring. A child brings an intense attitude of curiosity and delight as he or she explores. We can empathize with the child's curiosity and delight. As we watch we ask, Isn't there much that I too can find out?

As we cultivate wonder we sense deep down, instinctively, the imprint of a God who cares and cares very deeply. *Beware of anything that takes the wonder out of the life of a child!*

As teachers we need to constantly anticipate and plan for possible moments of awe, wonder, and delight. We can approach life with wonder and reverence.

Second, our classrooms need a climate of love and acceptance. Love is within all of us, yet human beings are born with a potential for love, not love itself. Love is a learned experience. This implies that if we have never had a model or the experience of love we literally don't know how to love even though we have the potential inside. This is why it is so important to demonstrate love to children. However, this love doesn't have to be cloying and always serious. It needs playful acts and words as well.

We can make this love personal in our classrooms. The fact that our Sunday school classes are usually not so large as our public school classrooms can be a benefit. Each person can be made to feel significant, important, special, and loved.

To welcome, to appreciate, to listen, to allow our students to speak with their own unique voices can be a way of teaching love.

Third, our classroom climate should be imaginative. If we have been matter of fact about our Sunday school teaching, let's try new methods. We want to open windows into another dimension of life. Our educational program must do everything it can to lift the hearts of our students to undreamed possibilities and unquestioned power made available to us in God's Spirit.

This book suggests four approaches to learning that you may not have tried before.

1. We begin with imagination and fantasy, powerful yet often neglected tools for learning about feelings and meaning.
2. We study kinesthetics and movement with the assurance that the body has wisdom to teach that the mind knows not of.
3. We look at word and symbol as means of not higher education but deeper education.
4. We look at antithesis and paradox as a way of speaking about the holy and as a way of teaching wholeness in life.

Creative Methods are suggested with which you may or may not feel comfortable: games, movement, dance, imaging, storytelling, drama.

All of these are offered with the understanding that experiences with God cannot be made, they just happen. But for persons to draw near to God they have to hear about the possibility of such an experience. They need to be given means to interpret, to appreciate the event. We plan experiences as pointers to deeper meaning. We offer the setting—

— and hope
— and pray
— and wait
— and allow time for God to act.

We acknowledge God's presence. We do not presume to know about, or have control over, God's interaction with our student.

As we seek ways to have a classroom climate of imagination there is no point at which we can say, "I have done enough." The memory of the persistent love of God that would not quit no matter what, drives us to try one more thing.

Wonder, love, imagination. In this climate, the church educational program points beyond the classroom to God and to the Christ as the source of its life.

PART I   IMAGINATION/FANTASY

IMAGINATION/FANTASY

Introduction

Stories and Experiences for Pre-School Children

        Experience 1: The Sparrow

        Experience 2: The Christmas Stable

        Experience 3: Weather Story

        Experience 4: Mixing the Senses

        Experience 5: Let's Pretend

        Experience 6: Three-Voice Story

Stories and Fantasizing with Scripture for Elementary Children

        Experience 7: Healing the Lame Man

        Experience 8: Rich Young Ruler

        Experience 9: Transfiguration

Imaging

        Experience 10: Imaging When You Are Tired

        Experience 11: Imaging to Solve Problems

        Experience 12: Imaging to Tap Resources of Strength

        Experience 13: Imaging to Help You Handle Grief

Creative Art Displays

        Experience 14: Palm Sunday Rock Display

        Experience 15: Look at Imaginary Creatures

Drama

        Experience 16: Meet the Monsters!

Resemblances

The world is that which cannot be known. The world is that which we each imagine.

Introduction

In this section we will be looking at understanding our faith through imagination and fantasy. We are consistently trained, throughout our lives, to solve problems by reasoning. In contrast, cultivation of the imagination is given little or no emphasis except in early childhood. What a shame.

Imagination can help us picture in the mind what is not apparent to the physical senses. It is the faculty by which we perceive what we have not observed by experience.

Imagination gives us a haunting power over time. The joy of living fully through our senses is preserved for us by our own ability to duplicate them in our imaginations. We savor life, tasting and retasting, seeing and reseeing through imagination. Imagination can give us strength for Christian living by helping us postpone satisfaction, denying ourselves for the sake of others, believing in the existence of what cannot be seen, giving us hope for eternal life. Imagination has great power to change lives by giving us personal insights. Fantasy can bring about renewed energy and a renewed capacity for achieving inner serenity. I read this arresting statement years ago and it has stuck in my mind:

From a child's capacity to imagine grows the adult's capacity for compassion.

How can we "teach" toward imagination and fantasy?

The capacity for fantasy is inherent in all humans. It can be fostered and encouraged, and this is our exciting opportunity in the church school.

The human imagination is still one of the great untapped resources for developing the growing child's ability to learn. At eighteen months and sometimes before, children show signs of make-believe in their play. What is more, the life of our eldest church member is enriched and deepened by experiences of imagination and fantasy.

STORIES AND EXPERIENCES FOR PRE-SCHOOL CHILDREN

Stories are a wonderful way to develop the imagination. They seem to have been a part of human history from the earliest beginning. An ancient legend says that the storyteller was created by a kind God to keep humankind from becoming weary-hearted with the burdens of daily living.

Jesus was a gifted storyteller, using vivid images: a man attacked by thieves, a son who returned home, a wedding feast. Creating visual pictures for our hearers is one of our tasks as church school storytellers.

For our purpose here, we want to emphasize the feeling and intuitive aspect of the biblical story so that it is not just another story to entertain and amuse. We want to present marvelous Bible stories in a way that will make an impact on our students, help them open their imaginations and internalize the heart of the story, help children achieve the serenity that is their right.

The following two stories can be used during a rest period in a Mother's Day Out program or after an active session in church school. The purpose is to open the imagination so as to sensitize a child to God.

Experience 1: The Sparrow

Gather the children around you. Give each child a feather. If these are feathers you have gathered together on a walk in the woods, or the students have brought into class, all the better. Just let the children stroke the feather and look at it and wonder. Then ask the children to close their eyes as they continue to touch and feel their feather while you tell them this story.

The Sparrow

Once Jesus said God watches every bird. His eye is on the sparrow, a tiny little brown bird.

Imagine you are flying like that little bird, high up in the quiet blue sky. You find a soft, fluffy white cloud and you let yourself sink down in it. Just feel that cloud all around you. It is fluffy and comfortable. So soft, so quiet, so high.

Hear God saying very quietly and gently, "I love every little creature and I especially love you."

Slowly stretch out your wings. Wave them gently in the air and then through the cool, blue sky fly back here and open your eyes.

There is something soothing about stroking a feather. Touch is especially important to pre-schoolers because it is their primary way of communication. In telling this story, you will want your voice to be soft and gentle. Speak slowly and dreamily. Leave pauses for the children to create the pictures in their minds. Suggest your children let their eyes look up even though closed. (When young children are looking down with closed eyes they tend to open their eyes, to peep around.)

Experience 2: The Christmas Stable

Ask the children to bring from home any stuffed animal they have that is like an animal that might have been in the stable when Jesus was born. Most have a woolly cat, lamb, or dog. One child in our class had a wonderful, soft, floppy camel. We included horses and chickens too and a cow puppet. Put the soft animals on a table around which the children sit, so that each child is within reach of a soft, furry creature to stroke. Tell the children to close their eyes. They can lay their heads on the table if they want to.

The Christmas Stable

It had been a long day for the new-born baby Jesus. It was the very first day of his life. In the warm stable near his mother and father, he listened to the quiet, quiet world.

Then he heard a tiny, soft rustling sound and felt something very soft and furry. "Good night, baby Jesus. We are glad you were born." It was the little kitten in the stable. Baby Jesus touched the soft fur.

"Good night, baby Jesus. We are glad you were born." It was the gentle-eyed cow mooing.

For a while all was quiet again. Then: "Good night baby Jesus. We are glad you were born." All the little lambs baah-ed together.

There was a tiny flutter of little wings and all the birds and chickens said, "Good night baby Jesus. We are glad you were born."

The stable was very quiet except for the gentle breathing of the animals.

Then: "Good night baby Jesus. We are glad you were born," said the camel in a funny, deep voice.

Then it was quiet for a long, long time. Baby Jesus touched his soft animal friends. All were asleep in the dark, quiet stable.

Then a sunbeam peeped through the cracks in the stable. The animals got up. Baby Jesus smiled. Another day was beginning.

Open your eyes now children.

Add a "good night" for each of the animals the children bring.

Experience 3: Weather Story

In this story the children act out movements to accompany the story. The teacher may beat a rhythm on a tambourine. A large open space is needed. Children may take off their shoes.

Note: If you live in an area that does not experience snow you may wish to substitute rain and wind.

Weather

God made every kind of weather, and it is wonderful what God can do.

In the winter God makes dancing snowflakes. Can we all move lightly and slowly, dancing softly like a snowflake?*(pause)*

Now lie on the floor. Pretend the ground is covered with deep snow. How would you roll in the snow?*(pause)*

Stand up again. The wind blows cold in God's winter. Pull your coat tight around you. Pull down your hat. Cover your ears. Are you shivering?*(pause)*

In the spring God makes soft raindrops to wake up the earth. Dance around like raindrops.*(pause)*

Now you are wading through puddles left by the rain.*(pause)*

Sit on the floor and curl up in a tight ball. You are a little seed. God sends sunshine to awaken you and you start to grow.*(pause)*

Grow and reach and stretch.*(pause)*

In the spring God's birds start to sing too. Be little birds flying around.*(pause)*

Often in the spring we get windy days. Feel the wind blowing you from side to side. Feel a gentle wind, a strong wind.*(pause)*

In God's summer the sun beats down very hot. Be a big shining sun.*(pause)*

It is fun to go barefooted and wiggle our toes in the sand.*(pause)*

But how do we walk barefooted on a hot sidewalk?*(pause)*

In the summer we swim in the cool water.*(pause)*

In God's autumn, leaves turn color and fall to the ground. Use your hands to show the leaves falling from the branches and fluttering and floating to the ground.*(pause)*

The leaves pile up on the ground and the wind blows them around. Can you dance like leaves being blown by the wind?*(pause)*

Sometimes there are foggy days. How do we walk in fog?*(pause)*

Thank you, God, for all kinds of weather.

From three years of age on, children can be storytellers. Explain to your class that the people of the early church told stories about Jesus. Give opportunities often in your classroom for the students to tell you Bible stories and encourage them to tell the stories to their parents and friends. This is a neglected skill we can develop.

A six-year-old child wrote the following story. The children were told to spell the words as best they could so as not to inhibit the flow of thought. (Spelling has been corrected by the editor.) Already at six, this little girl knew many parts of the Easter story.

Easter Story
by Christy Watson

Around Easter and in the month of April it is very special to Christians. It is sad and happy when Jesus rode into Jerusalem. Was happy the last supper, was sad after it was over. Jesus went into the garden of Gethsemane to pray. Then Judas led a group of people into the garden. The people took Jesus. Peter followed them. Peter denied Jesus three times before the rooster crowed. On Good Friday Jesus died on the cross. On Easter day he rose from the dead. Our God in life and death and life beyond death.

What are some other things to do that help to nurture the imagination of a very young child? The child may look at

1. his or her face in a mirror
2. a kaleidoscope

3. a piece of colored glass held up to a window
4. sea shells
5. Jack Frost's painting on a window on a frosty morning.

Ask the children to tell you what they see. Let them make up a story about it. How is God present in the story?

Experience 4: Mixing the Senses

An imagination stretcher that is fun for children is mixing the senses. The teacher tells the following action story as the children listen and participate.

Jesus Loves Children

Jesus was teaching the people on the gently sloping hillside beside the Sea of Galilee. The hillside was covered with flowers of every shape and color, and the Sea of Galilee was sky blue with silver sparkling waves. Some mothers brought their little children to Jesus and asked him to bless them. Jesus loves little children, so he took them in his arms and put his hands on their heads and prayed.

One of the children was wearing a beautiful blue dress. When I say "Go!" touch as many blue things in this room as you can find.

Go! *(children run around touching blue things)*

Now come back and sit around me. How many blue things did you touch? *(children respond)*

Think of blue and name all the things that smell like blue. *(accept all answers)*

Jesus took one of the little babies in his arms. The baby felt very, very soft. When I say "Go!" touch as many soft things in the room as you can find. *(children touch soft objects)*

Come back and sit around me. How many soft things did you touch? *(accept all answers)* What color feels soft? *(accept all answers)*

One of the children gave Jesus a juicy yellow pear. When I say "Go!" run and touch everything that is yellow.

Come back and sit around me. How many things did you touch? What kinds of things taste yellow?

One child gave Jesus a bright red flower he had picked. Jesus smelled it and smiled. Run and touch everything in the room that is red.

Come sit around me. How many things did you touch that were red? What are some things that sound red?

No one is ever incorrect in this game. Accept all answers and encourage the children to be free and spontaneous in their thinking.

Colors are one of the first concepts a child learns. Sometimes colors have specific meanings for children and sometimes they connect the visual sense and another of the senses such as tasting, smelling, or hearing as we did in the story above.

To further develop the imagination you can make this into a game by asking the children to associate objects and feelings with colors.

From a paint store get a booklet of paint samples. Some colors of paint have wonderfully suggestive names. Display a color, read the name, and ask the children to respond with an object or feelings.

Some unusual paint names from my store include:

amber	amethyst	apricot
azure	carmine	cinnabar
dawn	ebony	fuchsia
heliotrope	lapis lazuli	lavender
melon	oyster	pearl
pinto	pistachio	plum
raven	roan	russet
sanguine	tawny	titian
verdigris	vermilion	

After this game consider with your class how God has filled the world with shades and layers of color for our enjoyment and pleasure. God is the source of all beauty. We feel a satisfaction in thinking about and looking on beautiful things. "Fill your minds with those things that are good and that deserve praise," Paul said. Can we train our minds to think on lovely things?

Experience 5: Let's Pretend

Another way to nurture the imagination of pre-schoolers is through pretending and make-believe. Children love to pretend to be grown up.

The children can meet the church staff. The minister, robed if this is your custom, can go with the children to the sanctuary and show the children the pulpit and the baptismal font. If possible let the children use as many of their senses as they can by feeling the water, smelling the candles and flowers, seeing the colors and windows. The children can meet the church musician in this same fashion, perhaps touching the organ keys and hearing the sounds. The adults can show and tell the children what they do during the worship service.

Back in their Sunday school room the children pretend to be the adults they have just met. One pretends to be the minister, mimicking his or her acts. Another child pretends to be the musician. The whole class "plays church." This helps children build an awareness of the different persons they see at church and what their roles are. Role-playing occupations is a natural way to encourage pretend play.

Another time the teacher may say, Let's pretend we are going to church. How do we get ready? This should be a realistic game based on the child's awareness of his or her surroundings. Talk to the children about what you see on the way to church and when you get there.

Who do they see at church and what are they doing? The teacher is a leading player in this game. The children will need someone to guide them through the first few times.

Missionary stories are another way to broaden our children's background and imagination. After a visit to your classroom from a missionary, children can pretend to be the missionaries, doing their work as they understand it.

Experience 6: Three-Voice Story

Hand claps help identify the characters in this Bible story. Instructions:
1. Clap the tips of the fingers on one hand against the heel of the palm of the other hand. This is the voice of Samuel.
2. With stiff hands clap the palms together. This is Eli.
3. Cup your palms and clap them together. This is God.
4. After experiencing the story, go back and try to review the story with hand claps only. The first time prompt the children with a key phrase when they need it. Then see if you can do the story without any words.

I Samuel 1–3

Samuel was a special little boy. His mother, Hannah, promised to lend him to the Lord. So when he was still very young Samuel went to live with Eli, the high priest. Eli promised to take care of Samuel and teach him to serve God.

One night God spoke to Samuel. Now it had been a long, long time since anyone had heard God's voice. Samuel did not understand that God was speaking to him. He was only a child and he did not know very much about God.

He heard a voice calling him through the darkness. "Samuel! Samuel!" *(make God-claps).*
Samuel thought it was Eli calling him. So he rose quickly and ran to Eli.
  "Here I am," he said *(Samuel-claps).*
Eli was surprised.
  "I did not call for you my boy. Lie down again" *(Eli-claps).*
Soon the voice of God spoke again.
  "Samuel!" *(God-clap).*
Samuel rubbed his sleepy eyes and hurried again to Eli's bed. *(Eli-clap).*
Once more Eli said,
  "I did not call. Return to your bed" *(Eli-clap).*
The voice of God spoke a third time.
  "Samuel! Samuel!" *(God-clap).*
Again Samuel ran to Eli.
  "You called again" *(Samuel-clap).*
Eli understood that perhaps God was wishing to speak to his little friend. So he told Samuel to return to bed and say,
  "Speak, your servant is listening" *(Eli-clap).*
Samuel went back and lay down again and soon he heard the voice of God calling.
  "Samuel! Samuel!" *(God-clap).*
And he answered,
  "Speak, your servant is listening" *(Samuel-clap).*
And God talked with Samuel that night and told him he would be a great prophet.

STORIES AND FANTASIZING WITH SCRIPTURE FOR ELEMENTARY CHILDREN

As we move up through various grade levels we should continue to tell our stories as creatively as possible. A good starting point with elementary age children is to say,

"Pretend you are there and tell me in your own words what happened." For example, when studying the following stories you might say:

— Pretend you are in Jericho with Zacchaeus
— Pretend you are on the parade route on Palm Sunday
— Pretend you are there when Jesus heals the blind man
— Pretend you are with the children of Israel crossing the Sea of Reeds
— Pretend you are there when David slays Goliath.

Make up your own sentences for the stories you are telling. Use fantasizing with Scripture as in the following three stories.

Experience 7: Healing the Lame Man

If we neglect the feeling or intuitive aspect of a biblical passage then the story remains just another story. We miss the opportunity of internalizing the heart of the story and we lose the impact the story can make.

In this experience we take a scene from the life of Christ and relive it, taking part in it as if it were actually occurring and we were participants.

Begin by reading Luke 5:17-26 aloud. Lower the lights in the classroom. Have the students sit apart from one another and quiet themselves in preparation for the story.

Healing the Lame Man

We are using fantasy to attain a truth beyond fantasy. Using our imaginations we are going to put ourselves in this scene we have just read.

Imagine yourself in a small house in a crowded room with Jesus. Feel the people pushing, shoving, and jostling to get closer to Jesus. Look around at this crowd. See ill persons pushing through the crowd to be healed. See persons with wonder, amazement, and a little fear in their eyes. See Pharisees looking for fault in Jesus.

Look at Jesus in the center of all these people, quiet, serene. His disciples stand in a circle around him, protecting him as much as they can from the push of the crowd.

Hear a new sound. It is a scraping, tearing noise. See Jesus continuing his quiet ministry. Look up, with the rest of the crowd, and see the sky showing through a hole in the roof. See, directly over Jesus' head, a strange contraption being lowered through the roof. It is a makeshift pallet being lowered by ropes at each end. You can just make out the hands of four men lowering the pallet. It wobbles and bobs jerkily toward the floor. You recognize the man on the pallet. He is a crippled man whose face is puckered with pain and suffering. You are amazed and stretch forward to get a better look at Jesus to see what he will do. The pallet lands on the floor with a thud directly in front of Jesus. The crowd shifts to make room.

See Jesus smiling at the man. Hear his voice, "Son, your sins are forgiven." You are astonished. How can anyone forgive sins? You hear whispering around you, "Only God can forgive sins." There is a feeling of fear in the crowd.

Jesus seems to be looking directly at you. "Is it easier to tell the man that his sins are forgiven or to tell him to rise up from his bed and walk?" You feel that Jesus has seen

24

directly into your heart and that he knows the secrets that are there. You feel that your sins too are forgiven.

The crippled man stirs. He flexes his stiff limbs. He tests the new strength in his body. Now see him rising, standing. He rolls up the pallet and lifts it to his shoulder.

From the roof comes a great cheer from his friends. The surprised crowd makes way for him and he walks straight and strong through their midst into the street to join his happy friends.

You fall in behind him, leaving the house, the crowd, Jesus. Great amazement is upon the people in that crowded house. You feel it too. "Surely we have seen strange things today."

Continue walking until the house and people are far behind you. When you feel ready open your eyes.

Experience 8: Rich Young Ruler

Read Mark 10:17-23 together. Have the class close their eyes, take several deep breaths, and relax.

The Rich Young Ruler

Imagine that you are entering the scene you have just read. Picture the hillside where Jesus has been teaching. He is leaving. See in your mind the crowds of people getting up, walking away, conversing with one another. See children skipping around their mothers.

Jesus and his disciples are starting down the road away from the crowd when a young man rushes up to them. Picture the young man in your mind. His clothes are very rich. With your fingertips imagine the feel of velvet and silk. See his handsome face, and proud carriage.

He bows in the dust before Jesus, ignoring his rich clothes. Imagine the dust rising around him, settling on his clothes and face.

Hear his strong confident voice as he addresses Jesus, "Good Master, what good thing shall I do that I may receive life in the other world?" See Jesus looking straight at the young man. The man rises and they face each other, eye-to-eye. Hear Jesus reciting the commandments and the young man nodding impatiently.

"Yes, yes, I know the commandments of Moses and I have kept them all from my childhood. But I seem to lack something yet. O Master, tell me what it is."

Now see Jesus looking at the young man with great tenderness and love. Imagine you are that person and Jesus is looking at you. Hold the picture of Jesus' face in your mind. He is looking at you with great tenderness and love.

Hear Jesus' voice: "You lack one thing, just one. Go home, sell all that you have and give your riches to the poor . . . then come back and be my disciple."

See the young man avert his eyes from Jesus' gaze. See him turn away. His shoulders droop. His walk is slow. Without a word he walks away from Jesus. He is sad and deeply troubled.

See Jesus watching him walk away. Jesus stretches out his hand but the young man doesn't see. In your imagination follow the man until he is out of sight. See Jesus turning to look at you again and hear him speak, "And you?" React in any way that seems natural.

When you are ready open your eyes.

As a follow-up activity write a paragraph about the rich young man in his old age remembering that day. Is he bitter and cynical? Was he present at the crucifixion? Did he ever become a disciple? Have the riches of his youth satisfied him? Is he still searching for something?

Experience 9: Transfiguration

Begin by reading Matthew 17:1-13. Lower the lights in your classroom. Have students sit apart from one another.

The Transfiguration

Using our imaginations we are going to put ourselves in this scene.

You are climbing a mountain. It is a long, hard climb up a rough slope. You continue upward although your legs are beginning to ache. Soon you are far above the quiet valley below. The peak of the mountain is directly before you. There, on a level place, you see Jesus kneeling in prayer.

You stop a little way off and watch. You feel great power coming from Jesus as he prays. As you watch, his face begins to shine as the brightness of the sun; his clothing, too, gleams as white as snow. You can feel the great strength and tremendous power radiating from his body.

Before your eyes two other figures seem to materialize. They too glow with great brightness. From deep inside you, you recognize the figures as Moses and Elijah. You gaze in amazement at the glorious scene before you. In spite of the brightness, you do not have to shield your eyes. You feel no fear, only great awe.

As you continue to watch, a bright cloud descends upon the scene. You are caught in it. Sight becomes misty. The figures fade. You seem to hear a voice saying, "This is my own dear Son, with whom I am pleased." You stand motionless. Time seems to have stopped. You feel yourself trembling. You fall to the ground.

Then slowly the bright cloud rises. You see Jesus again where he was praying before. Now he is alone. He turns and looks at you. He speaks, "Rise up and do not be afraid."

You rise and start back down the mountain thinking about what you have seen.

When you are ready open your eyes.

There are several ways to follow up these fantasy stories.
1. Getting the inner picture out and on paper by drawing helps make the experience concrete.
2. Acting out the scene of the meditation may work in some groups.
3. Creative writing as mentioned after story 2.
4. Creating a symbol for the experience.

A woman in one of my workshops told me her story of how using the Bible in the manner of these three stories can influence your life.

She was sitting quietly reading the Bible story of the murder of the children by Herod, following Jesus' birth. She had had families from Nicaragua living in her home the past year. They had told about the mothers whose children were kidnapped. The connection came as she sat alone in silence reading her Bible. What would be helpful?

She decided that someone to stand with these mothers would help and she went to Nicaragua with a peace group for that purpose. She had felt so much a part of the Bible story she was reading that reaction in her daily life seemed a natural response.

As we use stories to develop the imagination, we find within the stories power that informs our life with creative meaning.

IMAGING

A powerful way to teach through imagination and fantasy is by the use of imagery. In imagery you think visually. Imaging is a step beyond putting yourself in a Bible story. You create in your mind a solid and realistic image or situation. It is not unlike daydreaming. If you daydream about something you hope to accomplish and you see these things in a positive manner you are using imagery. Elementary children can image easily. Their young minds seem more flexible, more ready to accept new ideas. Teenagers are aware of the use of imagery in sports training: tennis, basketball, skiing. Many coaches have teams visualize a perfect shot, a perfect form, and success follows.

Although your Sunday school class is a good group to practice imagery with, the traditional Sunday school setting does not seem best for this kind of learning. You need a quiet setting. You need an uninterrupted period of time. If you are with your class on an over-night trip or in a camp, imagery can work well.

Here are some steps to take as you begin to use imagery with your class.

1. Begin by having the class relax and close their eyes. Ask the members to visualize a peaceful scene *(allow 30 seconds of uninterrupted quiet)*.
2. Ask the class to add details to their scene: smells, sounds, colors *(30 seconds)*.
3. Ask the class, How many were able to do this?

Exercises like this will help you strengthen and stimulate your visual memory and make imaging possible. Suggesting ways to relax wrists, ankles, and neck helps to prepare the class physically.

How can imagery help members of your class? In a number of ways. Let's look at a few:

Experience 10: Imaging When You Are Tired

(Older Elementary and Youth)

I Will Mount Up with Wings as Eagles

Visualize a beautiful valley with sharp, steep mountains surrounding it *(30 seconds)*.

See an eagle soaring up from the valley to the mountain heights in wide circles. Feel the strength in the eagle's wings as it pulls upward. Visualize the feathers and the sharp, piercing eyes and the strength in the talons. Feel the wings hunch forward. Feel the strength increase. Imagine the power as the eagle mounts into the air currents. Feel the air currents carrying the eagle into a swooping, gliding pattern.

I Will Run and Not Be Weary

Imagine yourself running with a smooth rhythmic stride and the wind whistling around you. Your heart beats steadily. Feel the blood pulsing through your body. Your legs stretch to cover great distances. You almost bounce as you touch the ground. Your head is thrown back. You are breathing gulps of invigorating air. You run lightly, smoothly, swiftly, effortlessly.

I Will Walk and Not Faint

You are in a wide meadow alone. The sun is shining. Tall yellow grass surrounds you. You are walking with long, rhythmic strides. A strong walking cane helps support you. You can see for a great distance. You begin to walk the distance. One stride then another and another. You swing along, tirelessly, one foot following the other in a steady pattern. Power and strength are with you. Your breathing is slow and steady and deep. You know you can keep on and on and on. You walk tall and rhythmically.

Experience 11: Imaging to Solve Problems

(Youth)

Imaging helps you solve problems and make decisions. Imagining things permits a trial-and-error approach without assessing any penalty for error. It allows you to extrapolate the probable consequences of alternative decisions.

Here is a sample case. Cindy was adopted. In her high school years she had an opportunity to join a group that searched for their birth parents. Cindy was not sure if she wanted to do this or not.

She imaged in this way. She visualized herself joining the group. She thought about the meeting place and tried to add details until she could see it clearly in her mind. She saw herself in the group meeting. Then she visualized in detail telling her adoptive parents what she had done. She imaged their response. She considered several possible responses and tried to image the situation as clearly as possible. She added colors, touches, smells, and so forth.

She tried to imagine herself in the future and the future responses that would follow her decision. She tried to consider every possible angle in her mind. Instead of saying, "Is this right, or is this right?" she just imaged herself in both situations.

After doing this a number of times, she realized one direction seemed clearer. She had not rushed impulsively into an error but had allowed imagery to help her decide. It helped her take the risk of deciding and committing herself to one among many possibilities.

I don't know how this works, but it seems that in imagery the mind relaxes. It stops fretting over a problem and you seem to become more receptive to flashes of insight. This is one of the best ways to help children and youth achieve self-direction. Imagery can help us face the unknown future in an original, venturesome, and independent manner. Imaging, far from being an escape into illusion, is a way the mind playfully explores alternatives.

Here is a hint. When we are trying to visualize something that has happened in the past, the eyes generally tend to go up and to the left. In the future they go up and to the right. Try it.

Experience 12: Imaging to Tap Resources of Strength

(Older Elementary and Youth)

Modern life tends to dull our senses and inhibit creativity. Finding bits and pieces of rich experiences, such as these times of imaging, balances our lives and prepares us for Christian learning and living.

Psalm 23:1-3

First read Psalm 23:1-3. Empty your mind of irritation, worry, and frustration.

Say slowly: The Lord is my Shepherd. I have everything I need. He lets me rest in the field of green grass and leads me to quiet pools of fresh water. He gives me new strength.

Imagine yourself walking in a green pasture. Smell the fresh new grass. Let your eyes relax as they gaze on the soft green. Feel the grass beneath your feet and brushing your ankles. You are feeling calm and tranquil. Walk slowly, absorbing the scene with all your senses; smell the fragrances.

As you walk you come to a pool of water. Look deep into its depths. It is still and peaceful. You cannot see the bottom, only layer upon layer of deep still water.

You feel completely satisfied. You repeat the words, "I have everything I need." You feel protected, loved, and at peace.

Now, from deep within, you feel strength arising. From these tranquil settings, pastures and still water, pictured in your mind, draw strength. Let the scenes of nature restore you. Feel yourself as strong as the earth itself, as tenacious as grass. Feel your strength as deep as bottomless pools of water. Know the assurance of being protected by a great Shepherd. Be calm and strong.

Experience 13: Imaging to Help You Handle Grief

Do Not Be Worried and Upset

Read John 14:1-2. Begin with long, slow, deep breaths. Put yourself in a favorite place. It may be a beautiful garden. Become aware of the lovely things around you—birds singing, sun shining, the fragrance of flowers.

Imagine that the person who has just died is here with you in this beautiful place. Recall your affection and love for this person. Take as long as you want with this.

Now visualize the funeral and burial of this person. Watch it again in your mind as it happened, but view it with tranquility, peace, and love. Hear Jesus speaking to you. Do not be worried and upset.

Say good-bye to the loved one in any way that feels right to you. Feel assured that this person is going to a dwelling place of beauty. Let the person go.

Turn and walk back to your beautiful garden. Feel calm and confident. Surround yourself with the strength and faith Jesus taught. Repeat the words of John 14:1-2 over and over to yourself.

In death there is a grief scarcely paralleled by all other misfortunes of life. We need help in dealing with this separation.

We have looked at four examples of imaging:

1. to work out fatigue
2. to solve problems
3. to tap buried resources of strength
4. to handle grief

Imagery can be used powerfully in other ways also. It can add color and liveliness to our lives. Sometimes we can overcome the ache of loneliness by engaging in imagery. It can be used to make us confident, optimistic, positive persons. Creative imaging renews our vitality and restores our souls.

CREATIVE ART DISPLAYS

Art is a good medium for developing fantasy and imagination.

Experience 14: Palm Sunday Rock Display

(Elementary, Youth, or Intergenerational)

Following is a Palm Sunday suggestion for an entire Sunday school or a specific class. It may be carried out by elementary Sunday school classes, youth groups, or intergenerational groups.

A project such as this is good for developing imaging and imagination skills for a number of reasons.

1. It encourages individual expression.
2. It allows children to reach deep into inner images and gain insights for their creation.
3. It enables children to consider Palm Sunday in a new way.
4. It asks questions that search for meaning in a nonthreatening way.
5. It allows sharing when the display is completed.

Palm Sunday is a special day in the church and church school. It marks the beginning of Holy Week. We recall the story of a royal procession. We recall the day of the triumphant entry of Jesus into Jerusalem before his trial and death (Luke 19:28-40).

In the drama and pageantry that accompanies the celebration of Palm Sunday we dwell on palm branches and hosannas and sometimes overlook a short sentence in the biblical narrative. It is Luke 19:40: "I tell you that if they keep quiet, the stones themselves will start shouting." Listen to the story.

The Palm Sunday Parade

Jesus was on the Palm Sunday donkey, descending the Mount of Olives, when a whole multitude began to rejoice and praise God with a loud voice. The enthusiasm grew and so did the noise. Children squealed with glee, and voices became shriller and more penetrating. Indignant, some of the Pharisees edged alongside Jesus: their eyebrows furrowed, their mouths in tight lines. Trying to keep their stride dignified as they kept pace with the clippety-clop of the donkey, they spoke disapprovingly to Jesus: "Teacher, rebuke your disciples."

Then Jesus replied, like in the verse from Luke, "I tell you that if they keep quiet, the stones themselves will start shouting."

This verse becomes the focus for an art project to be displayed in your church narthex or Sunday school hall during Holy Week.

You will be making a Palm Sunday procession trail populated by "rock people." Needed are small rocks of various shapes that can stand alone or be glued together to suggest figures. Part of your project could be to have the group go outdoors and select a rock of their choice, of whatever size or shape.

Then have on hand wire, string, yarn, felt scraps, epoxy glue, button eyes, glitter, pipe cleaners, and whatever else your imagination or Sunday school supply closet suggests. You will need acrylic paint, brushes, and markers also.

Read the Bible story again and ask the group to create one or more rock people who might have been in the Palm Sunday procession.

Yarn can become hair, buttons can become facial features. Felt-tipped pens can be used to suggest expressions. Felt scraps can become clothes. Several faces can be painted onto a single rock. The odd, original shape of the stone can suggest the nature of the face or grouping. A piece of felt attached to the bottom of the rock will prevent it from scuffing surfaces.

Ask the group to think about the emotions that might have been present in the people in that Palm Sunday group: excitement, joy, merriment, fear, doubt, indifference, worry, love, and so forth. Discuss the types of people who might have been in the crowd and what their feelings might have been. Try to visualize them. Will mouths be open in shouts? Will the enemies of Jesus be anywhere in the crowd?

There were certainly children. What would have been their feelings? How can they be portrayed? We know there were enemies of Jesus. Are there rock shapes that suggest hostility? Perhaps some were in the crowd who had had personal contact with Jesus through hearing his preaching or participating in a miraculous healing. What will their expressions be? And we know a procession or parade always attracts the simply curious. How will they be portrayed?

Give everyone ample time to create. Allow time for the rock people to dry. As the creations are drying the group might like to recall other times the word or symbol of a rock is used in the Bible.

Some passages are:

1. In the book of Psalms, the word *rock* is used to suggest safety: "He set me safely on a rock and made me secure" (Ps. 40:2).
2. In the book of Isaiah, God is seen as a mighty Rock: "Israel, you have forgotten the God who rescues you and protects you like a mighty rock" (Isa. 17:10*a*).
3. In the New Testament Jesus met Simon Peter and said, " 'Your name is Simon son of John, but you will be called Cephas.' (This is the same as Peter and means 'a rock')" (John 1:42).

4. In the book of Matthew, we find rock representing strength: "The rain poured down, the rivers flooded over, and the wind blew hard against that house. But it did not fall, because it was built on rock" (Matt. 7:25).

Think about what a rock is and why a rock is used in these passages. Would you like to be called "Rock"? A rock is an amalgam of various constituents resulting in strength and durability. For example, granite is made up of quartz, feldspars, and mica. None of these suggests strength to us when found alone, but when they are compounded, strength and durability are recognized. When the many components of our lives are consolidated to one purpose, strength results. We become rocks.

Piling up stones is an elementary form of leaving marks. There are many Old Testament illustrations of this. Erecting a monument is telling to anyone passing that here is an important spot, that somebody has been here before. That is our purpose in creating our Palm Sunday rock procession.

A table top with a sandy trail will suggest the setting for your Jerusalem journey. Group the completed rock people along the path. You may wish to make a long paper banner of the biblical words from Luke 19:40 to lie beside your path. The group might like to add other background to your scene.

When the display is finished you may want to have a simple dedication of the display. When all is ready and in place gather the class around the display and offer the following prayer.

Teacher:
O God, Our heavenly Parent and divine Ruler, like the crowds that pressed on Jesus on that first Palm Sunday, we often praise you with our lips only. Help us search within ourselves to discover where we stand in the crowd. Give us courage to be among those who respond from their hearts with shouts of praise and songs of joy. Open our lips.

Students:
And our mouths shall show forth thy praise. Praise God from whom all blessings flow. Praise him all creatures here below. Praise him above ye heavenly host. Praise Father, Son, and Holy Ghost.

Experience 15: Look at Imaginary Creatures

The hesitation to confront children with the supernatural aspects of the gospel story seems to stem from emphasis on people as rational beings whose destiny is largely in the hand of the individual.

As we seek to develop imagination as a tool for understanding God, let us meet these supernatural beings head on. There are many imaginative creatures described in the Bible.

To set the stage for this activity, read and ponder these words from Isaiah 55:8: "My thoughts," says the Lord, "are not like yours, and my ways are different from yours." Then focus on the following words from Scripture. Afterward, we will try to draw the beings the Scriptures describe.

Ezekiel 1:5-13

At the center of the storm I saw what looked like four living creatures in human form, but each of them had four faces and four wings. Their legs were straight, and they had hoofs like those of a bull. They shone like polished bronze. In addition to their four faces and four wings, they each had four human hands, one under each wing. Two wings of each creature were spread out so that the creatures formed a square, with their wing tips touching. When they moved, they moved as a group without turning their bodies.

Each living creature had four different faces: a human face in front, a lion's face at the right, a bull's face at the left, and an eagle's face at the back. Two wings of each creature were raised so that they touched the tips of the wings of the creatures next to it, and their other two wings were folded against their bodies. Each creature faced all four directions, and so the group could go wherever they wished, without having to turn.

Revelation 4:6b-9a

Surrounding the throne on each of its sides, were four living creatures covered with eyes in front and behind. The first one looked like a lion; the second looked like a bull; the third had a face like a man's face; and the fourth looked like an eagle in flight. Each one of the four living creatures had six wings, and they were covered with eyes, inside and out. Day and night they never stop singing:

"Holy, holy, holy, is the Lord God Almighty,
  who was, who is, and who is to come."

The four living creatures sing songs of glory and honor and thanks to the one who sits on the throne, who lives forever and ever.

Sing about supernatural beings. A possible hymn is "Let All Mortal Flesh Keep Silence." Look particularly at verse 4:

> At his feet the six-winged seraph,
> Cherubim, with sleepless eye,
> Veil their faces to the presence,
> As with ceaseless voice they cry,
> Alleluia, Alleluia,
> Alleluia, Lord most high.

Read about Leviathan the imaginary sea monster in Psalm 104:26.

Now draw the creatures described in these passages using all the imagination you can. Draw on a large roll of mural paper. Surround yourself with these imaginary beings by hanging the drawings up in your classroom.

The reasons for using these activities is to increase the understanding of the magnitude of God's world. In our culture our tendency to deify the merits of rationalism, though it does have merit, has caused us to ignore the value of the imagination. We can expand our concept of the universe as we emphasize the importance of thinking in and experiencing in images.

DRAMA

Drama is always good for imagination and fantasy because it allows many different interpretations including our own creative interpretation of an idea.

We will use drama to personify negative feelings in the next experience.

Experience 16: Meet the Monsters!

(Youth at Halloween)

Getting ready: A class of at least twelve is needed for this experience. If you have a smaller class, read the material yourself, or along with just a couple of student readers. Be sure to leave enough students to create the monsters. The program may be undertaken in one of two ways. Students may work out the monster movement with costumes, make-up, sound, and so forth. Or, the monsters may be created on the spot.

Meet the Monsters

Student 1 Wild and woolly things! Grotesque and gruesome creatures! Monsters! Today we see them in movies, television, cartoons, books, toys. What are they doing in church school?

There are some negative qualities that we, as humans, share with every four-footed animal. These are monsters of behavior that are lurking in us all. Today we will meet the monsters. We will identify them. Are they us? We will seek to capture them and then we will seek to neutralize them.

(A student runs up and hands the leader a note.)

Ladies and gentlemen, we interrupt this class for a special announcement. The monster has been sighted. It is here in this very area. The monster is Greed!

What do we know about this monster? Here is his monster M.O.:

— He wants more and more.
— He wants more than his rightful share.
— He has a great overwhelming desire to possess.
— He utters a frightful sound: *"Gimme! Gimme! Gimme!"*

We have an account of this monster back in Jesus' day. Listen to this story:

Student 2

Then Jesus told them this parable: "There was once a rich man who had land which bore good crops. He began to think to himself, 'I don't have a place to keep all my crops. What can I do? This is what I will do,' he told himself; 'I will tear down my barns and build bigger ones, where I will store the grain and all my other goods. Then I will say to myself, Lucky man! You have all the good things you need for many years. Take life easy, eat, drink, and enjoy yourself!' But God said to him, 'You fool! This very night you will have to give up your life; then who will get all these things you have kept for yourself?'"

(Luke 12:16-21)

Student 3 Now we will create this monster. Will a volunteer please come and stand in the middle of the room? Using just your body, and the floor if you wish, form any interesting shape that you can hold for a few minutes. Create a shape that suggests greed, such as grasping arms.

Now will a second person join the first, touching the first person so as to create a completely new shape?

(One by one other students join the growing human sculpture, always touching one member of the existing group yet adding their own particular shape. Students are instructed to aim for a shape that expresses greed. Use not more than six students or fewer than three for this monster. This may be rehearsed before time or done spontaneously.)

And here we have it! Be on the constant lookout for this monster!

(Pause here and discuss with your class why certain shapes were used.)

Student 4 A second monster has now appeared. We shall meet this monster too as we read a Bible story and then create. The second monster is Selfishness. This monster's M.O. is:

— He is self-centered.

— He cares too little for others.

Student 5

As Jesus was starting on his way again, a man ran up, knelt before him, and asked him, "Good Teacher, what must I do to receive eternal life?"

"Why do you call me good?" Jesus asked him. "No one is good except God alone. You know the commandments: 'Do not commit murder; do not commit adultery; do not steal; do not accuse anyone falsely; do not cheat; respect your father and your mother.' "

"Teacher," the man said, "ever since I was young, I have obeyed all these commandments."

Jesus looked straight at him with love and said, "You need only one thing. Go and sell all you have and give the money to the poor, and you will have riches in heaven; then come and follow me." When the man heard this, gloom spread over his face, and he went away sad, because he was very rich.

Jesus looked around at his disciples and said to them, "How hard it will be for rich people to enter the Kingdom of God!"

The disciples were shocked at these words, but Jesus went on to say, "My children, how hard it is to enter the Kingdom of God! It is much harder for a rich person to enter the Kingdom of God than for a camel to go through the eye of a needle."

At this the disciples were completely amazed and asked one another, "Who, then, can be saved?"

Jesus looked straight at them and answered, "This is impossible for man but not for God; everything is possible for God."

Then Peter spoke up, "Look, we have left everything and followed you."

"Yes," Jesus said to them, "and I tell you that anyone who leaves home or brothers or sisters or mother or father or children or fields for me and for the gospel, will receive much more in this present age. He will receive a hundred times more houses, brothers, sisters, mothers, children, and fields—and persecutions as well; and in the age to come he will receive eternal life. But many who are now first will be last, and many who are now last will be first."

(Mark 10:17-31)

Student 6 As with the first monster, Greed, we create this monster by having one person stand in the middle of the room and form a shape with his or her body that suggests selfishness. Think about this monster. Would the figure be more ingrown? more inward reaching? holding? grasping tightly? looking around fearfully as if someone would take something from it? What would its call be? "Mine! Mine! Mine!"?

(Other students should hook on to the central figure, creating the monster Selfishness. Use not more than six or fewer than three students. Try to use students other than those you used before. Ask the students why they chose the shapes they did to suggest selfishness.)

Student 7 Here is a truly frightful monster, Temper! Unfortunately, we all know what temper is!

Then Jesus went to Nazareth, where he had been brought up, and on the Sabbath he went as usual to the synagogue. He stood up to read the Scriptures and was handed the book of the prophet Isaiah. He unrolled the scroll and found the place where it is written,
> "The Spirit of the Lord is upon
> me,
> because he has chosen me to
> bring good news to the poor.
> He has sent me to proclaim
> liberty to the captives
> and recovery of sight to the blind,
> to set free the oppressed
> and announce that the time
> has come
> when the Lord will save his
> people."

Jesus rolled up the scroll, gave it back to the attendant, and sat down. All the people in the synagogue had their eyes fixed on him, as he said to them, "This passage of scripture has come true today, as you heard it being read."

They were all well impressed with him and marveled at the eloquent words that he spoke. They said, "Isn't he the son of Joseph?"

He said to them, "I am sure that you will quote this proverb to me, 'Doctor, heal yourself.' You will also tell me to do here in my hometown the same things you heard were done in Capernaum. I tell you this," Jesus added, "a prophet is never welcomed in his hometown. Listen to me: it is true that there were many widows in Israel during the time of Elijah, when there was no rain for three and a half years and a severe famine spread throughout the whole land. Yet Elijah was not sent to anyone in Israel, but only to a widow living in Zarephath in the territory of Sidon. And there were many people suffering from a dreaded skin disease who lived in Israel during the time of the prophet Elisha; yet not one of them was healed, but only Naaman the Syrian."

When the people in the synagogue heard this, they were filled with anger. They rose up, dragged Jesus out of town, and took him to the top of the hill on which their town was built. They meant to throw him over the cliff, but he walked through the middle of the crowd and went his way.

(Luke 4:16-30)

Do you know what this monster's call is? Listen—an angry roar.

(Before creating this monster in practice or spontaneously, discuss some hostile ways to hold your hands, arms, feet, and head. Create this monster in the same way you did the other two, with students having not yet participated, beginning with a central figure who creates a temper stance and other students who hook on to create a monster. The three monsters stand in the center of the room. They begin chanting these words:

36

"If you want to be a monster, here's your chance.
'Cause everybody's doing the monster dance."

The monsters move around making their monster noises. Use contemporary music if available.)

We laugh at monsters and think we are modern people who know better. Yet aren't greed, selfishness, and temper really monsters? Our demons have not disappeared. They merely have new names. Engage the class in identifying other monsters and demons we must encounter in today's world. Our defense against such monsters is the same as it was in Jesus' day. Listen to the words from Luke 6:18*b* and 19: "Those who were troubled by evil spirits also came and were healed. All the people tried to touch him, for power was going out from him and healing them all."

Resemblances

Through Imagination, Seeing Christ in Others

It is a strange and marvelous thing to see a resemblance, something in a child that reflects the parent. It is not a feature. It is something more nebulous, something fleeting, a mannerism or expression. Is it hereditary? Imitation? What does it mean?

When we get older we often realize that we look more like our parents though our frames and features are different. What is it that we see at such times? An unconscious gesture? A fleeting expression? An illusion? This is an ancient theme that plays through us.

Did those around Jesus pick up something? A shadow? A hint of the ancestors who lived within them?

We read in Christian literature about Christ "dwelling" within us. Have you ever seen it? Have you seen something of the Christ in others? A certain look out of the eyes, which is a clue to goodness and depth?

What a thought! That if we live close to Christ others could see a family resemblance.

Faith is opening ourselves to God so that the living Christ may be reflected in us. Faith opens our hearts to the indwelling of the Spirit of God so that we will show what it means to be created in the image of God.

PART II KINESTHETICS/MOVEMENT

KINESTHETICS/MOVEMENT

Introduction

Games for Pre-School Children

Experience 17: God the Creator
Experience 18: God Knows Your Name
Experience 19: God's Special Child
Experience 20: Love

Games for Elementary Children

Experience 21: God Is Ever Seeking Us
Experience 22: The Love of God Is a Free Gift to Us
Experience 23: God Is to Worship and Adore
Experience 24: We Respond by Opening Ourselves to God
Experience 25: God Comes in Covenant

Kinesthetic Tracing

Experience 26: Kinesthetic Tracing for Elementary Children
Experience 27: Kinesthetic Tracing for Pre-School Children

Dancing

Experience 28: Dancing Our Belief About Easter
Experience 29: Joy to the World
Experience 30: All Things Bright and Beautiful
Experience 31: Dance the News

Movement

Experience 32: Service for Holy Innocents Day
Experience 33: Movement Expresses Feelings

The body has wisdom to teach that the mind knows not of.

Introduction

The way that we will seek to know and understand God in this section is through movement and kinesthetics. We have the wonderful gift of bodies. These bodies are instruments we can train to obey us. Yet the body can also teach us. If we learn to listen to our bodies they will tell us when we need rest, or exercise, or food.

The way we stand, sit, move, and gesticulate communicates a great deal about how we are feeling. Sometimes we can assume the physical posture first and the feeling will follow. Remember the Walt Disney song "Give a Little Whistle"? The fearful person whistled and assumed bravery and the feeling (courage) followed the act (whistling).

In this book we are emphasizing feelings. For every type of emotion there is a common impulse to act or to move. There is a connection between feelings and movement. We bare teeth in anger, nuzzle to express affection, dance with delight.

Why don't we make use of our whole bodies on Sunday mornings? In a typical Sunday school class we need only ears, maybe a mouth, and occasionally a hand. How can we make better use of our whole bodies to explore the Bible and Christian principles? This section attempts to answer this question by helping you experience the connection between feelings and movement through games, movements, and dance.

The Bible recognizes the power of the body to communicate. For example, the story of Jesus kneeling to wash the disciples' feet communicates a powerful message about service. Often our bodies can say things our words cannot. A hug or a handshake at a time of sorrow is an example. In these situations the language of movement is both more powerful and more memorable than mere words can ever be.

In Sunday school I teach through games more and more. This great teaching method is really ours by default. Organized teams and sports for children and sedentary television viewing have dumped along the wayside play and games, which are tried and true methods children have used for learning for generations. We in the church have only to pick them up, to adopt them, to channel them. This idea occurred to me when I heard a teacher say, "Let's get our lesson done, then we can play a game."

I realized that the atmosphere around games is the atmosphere I like for learning: excitement, anticipation, laughing, sharing. Let's not wait until "the lesson is done" to create this kind of atmosphere.

Playing with children can be exhilarating for the teacher too, giving us a new sense of lightness and delight.

What is God like? Have you heard the story of the four blind men who attempted to describe an elephant? One felt the elephant's trunk and said, "An elephant is like this." Another felt the leg and said, "An elephant is like this." The third blind man felt the elephant's back and the fourth man felt its tail. Each described a part and spoke honestly, but none grasped the whole picture. In the same way our small minds cannot grasp the extent of the greatness of our God. But we can look at parts and say, "God is like this" and "God is like this." In the following experiences a statement describing some aspect of God will be presented to your class. Then the class will play a game in an attempt to experience this definition.

Access to truth about God that does not depend on factual knowledge is what we seek here. We seek an introduction to God. We seek a meeting with God. We seek an experiencing of God's Presence and Power.

The first four games are for pre-schoolers. As a result of the following experiences we hope the children will be able to describe what they think God is like. We will be working on forming images of God.

GAMES FOR PRE-SCHOOL CHILDREN

Experience 17: God the Creator

God filled the world with wonderful, marvelous creatures. Play this game:
1. Choose a leader.
2. The leader walks around the room with everyone in class following.
3. Suddenly the leader turns around and shouts a word (the name of some animal or creature). For example: "spider."
4. Everyone assumes a position like that word and freezes.
5. The best "spider" gets to be the next leader (or you may simply choose another leader).
6. Everyone follows the new leader and the game is played again.

After the game, read all or a portion of Psalm 104. Say a prayer: "Thank you God for creating a world with so many wonderful animals to enjoy." Spend some time memorizing the verse: "Lord, you have made so many things! How wisely you made them all" (Ps. 104:24).

Experience 18: God Knows Your Name

God knows every one of you by name. Each of you is special to God.

Play the game Clap, Clap:

1. Everyone sits in a circle.
2. Everyone claps two beats together.
3. And then everyone keeps quiet for two beats.
4. Practice until all have the rhythm.
5. Then in the space between claps someone calls out his name—Mark!
6. The group claps twice.
7. The next person calls out her name—Joy!
8. The group claps twice.
9. Continue around the circle until all names are said.

After the game say a prayer: "Thank you God for loving us. We know Jesus especially loved little children and that you do too. Thank you God for knowing our names. Amen."

Experience 19: God's Special Child

God chose you, just as you are, as his special child. Play this game of drawing faces:

1. Children sit in a circle of four around a table with paper and crayon.
2. Each child draws the head and hair only of the child on his or her right.
3. Then each drawing is moved counterclockwise to the next person and every child adds the eyes and the eyebrows of the original child.
4. The drawing is moved again and the nose of the original child is added.
5. The drawing is moved again and the mouth is added.
6. The picture is moved again, back to the child who began it. This child adds any extras: ribbons or ties or glasses or ears.
7. Move the picture again. Each picture should be in front of the child it illustrates. Class members hold up their pictures for all to see.

After the game, pray: "Thank you God for making each of us special. Thank you that there is no one on earth exactly like me. Thank you that all my friends are special too. Amen."

Experience 20: Love

God loves us and wants us to love one another. Follow these directions for the game Giving Away Kisses.

1. Children sit in a circle.
2. All chant together:

> First you kiss your hand
>   (children kiss back of their hands)
> That's a kiss for me
> Then you turn to a friend
> And put the kiss on their knee
>   (children give kiss to friend on his or her knee).

3. Make up different places to put kisses. Encourage children to make suggestions. Repeat the chant each time, changing the last word. If you feel creative add a rhyming line. For example:

> And put the kiss in their hair
> Now what's it doing there?
>
> or
>
> And put the kiss on their toe
> No one will ever know.
>
> or
>
> And put the kiss on their ear
> Because they are very dear.

After the game, Pray: "Thank you God for your love. Let us help you spread it around."

GAMES FOR ELEMENTARY CHILDREN

The games for elementary-aged children deal with more advanced concepts of what God is like. These games are followed by discussion.

Experience 21: God Is Ever Seeking Us

Gather the children together outdoors and play the game Red Rover with them.

Instructions:
Two teams line up facing each other. Each team holds hands to form a strong chain. One team shouts "Red Rover! Red Rover! Let_____ come over!" (call the name of the person from the other team you want to come over). The person whose name has been called runs to the line and tries to break through. The members of the team try to keep the runner from breaking through by holding tightly to each other's hands. If the runner succeeds in breaking through, he or she takes one of the players back to the other team. If the runner does not succeed, he or she stays with the opposing team. The teams alternate calling players to try and break through their line.
Play until one team has all the players.

Discussion:
After playing the game for a while, gather the children together around you and ask: "Why do you suppose we played this game at Sunday school today?" ("It was fun." "To see who is strong.")
"We are supposed to be studying about God at Sunday school. What could this game have to do with God?" (One suggestion I received was "God is strong.")
Let's sit quietly and let our minds think about this big idea. God loves you and created you for fellowship. More than anything God wants to come into your life. We do lots of things to keep God out. We ignore God. We aren't quiet long enough to hear God speak to us. But God is always here, very close to us.
God is always trying to break into our lives. That's why we played Red Rover. We held

our hands and arms tight so the other side couldn't break through. Sometimes we shut ourselves up and hold ourselves tight so God can't come in. But remember that God is not going to give up trying to come into our lives. No matter what. No matter how long we live. God is always very close to us.

God comes always seeking us. We must learn to open ourselves to God and trust the goodness of God.

Experience 22: The Love of God Is a Free Gift to Us

Ask, What is the best gift you have ever received? Each child decides on a present. Each child then decides how to act out a movement for that present. Give the children a few minutes to practice and then ask them to spread around the room and climb into imaginary boxes. One person is "it." "It" selects a present, carefully untying the box. The "present" acts out its movement. The rest of the class guesses what the present is.

Discussion:

Share the following ideas to stimulate questions and discussion. God seeks us and we do no more than receive the gracious gift. Faith or trust is our response to God. It comes as a gift. Will we receive the gift? Christian faith starts from the fact that God has been revealed to us in distinct ways, calling us into communion with God.

Experience 23: God Is to Worship and Adore

Before this game, practice two slow claps followed by three quick claps as you lead the class in reciting,

> Sing praise   to our king.
> Dance praise   to the Lord.

Play the game:
1. Form a circle of students. "It" stands in the middle.
2. Lead the class in a hand-clapping rhythm—two slow claps followed by three quick claps as all chant the words above.
3. "It" walks around the inside of the circle to the clapping rhythm and stops in front of somebody.
4. "It" does a simple step in time to the rhythm. This could include a jump, hop, kick, or rock on heels or toes, as everyone sings "Sing praise to our King."
5. The person in front of whom "It" is standing must try to repeat the steps on the phrase, "Dance praise to the Lord."

If the student misses, "It" moves around the circle and stops in front of someone else. The student who copies the steps correctly becomes the leader. The new leader may change the step or keep the same step.

Discussion:

To begin, share some ideas like the following.

Let's sit quietly and let our minds think about this big idea. We owe our existence and the nature of our being to someone else more powerful than ourselves. We did not call ourselves into being but were brought into being by someone else. We simply found ourselves in existence. Our purpose for being is to adore our Maker.

Is this a new idea for you? A main purpose in life is to adore and praise God. God created people in the image of God in order to enter into fellowship with them. Our chief end is to glorify God and enjoy God forever.

Experience 24: We Respond by Opening Ourselves to God

Faith is opening ourselves to God's own Spirit, to make ourselves ready and willing to be taken hold of by God's power and love. Words used to describe this experience fall short. The reality goes far beyond the meanings of words.

This game, Balloon Bounce, can be used with children as young as three years. I have included it in the section for elementary age children because they also enjoy it so much.

Untie an air-filled balloon but hold it by the neck. Throw it up in the air and see what happens. There will be a wild dance—dipping, twisting, turning, shooting, swoops, swerves, spurts, zooms, zips.

Ask children to be a balloon that loses its air. Remind the balloons that every part of them must move.

Discussion:

This is how we act when the breath of God goes out of us. We flip around without any direction or guidance. Not to have meaning in life is to flop and flutter out of control.

Experience 25: God Comes in Covenant

God told us, I will be your God, I want you for my people. Play the game Sculptor and Clay:

1. Divide the group into partners. One person is the sculptor, one is the clay. (Later they will swap roles.)
2. All begin with clay lying curled up in a ball.
3. The sculptor moves the clay. The clay has no will of its own and must stay the way it is put, allowing the sculptor to make all the decisions. The clay should be as relaxed as possible while the sculptor molds it and then should try to hold the final position.
4. The entire group views the finished work.
5. The sculptor and clay swap roles.

Discussion:

How did it feel to be clay? Was it easy to let someone else mold you? Which did you like best, being clay or sculptor? What are some ways we can let God mold us?

KINESTHETIC TRACING

Games are not the only way to use the body in learning. Let's look now at movement as a way to build our faith. There is a kind of muscle training, a skill whereby our muscles take over. If you learned to ride a bicycle as a child or ice-skate and then did not engage in the activity for many years, when you mount a bicycle again or strap on ice skates your muscles begin to "remember" the balance, the rhythm, the technique, and off you go.

As we consider using our whole bodies to learn about our faith, where can muscle training fit in?

Experience 26: Kinesthetic Tracing for Elementary Children

1. Say the phrase of Jesus, "I am the light of the world" (John 8:12).
2. Trace each letter on a blank piece of paper with your index finger.
3. Do this three times.
4. Then try to write it out with a pencil. You may find that your muscles can now "remember" how to write it.

If your children are very familiar with this verse, and can write it from memory, you can still use this verse for this experience.

1. Do not tell the children the words you will be tracing.
2. Explain that you will blindfold them and then take their finger and trace some words three times on a blank piece of paper. Then you will give them a pencil to repeat the movements.
3. Tell the children that as you do the tracing they should relax and let their hand "memorize" the movements.
4. Have the rest of the class turn away from the child you are working with so they do not have a chance to catch on to what words you are using. Or, use a different word or set of words for each child.

This is called "kinesthetic tracing." *Kine* is a Greek word that means "to move." *Esthetic* is another Greek word meaning "to understand." So learning to remember by tracing is learning to understand through movement.

Read with your class the context in which Jesus stated "I am the light of the world" (John 8). Jesus was teaching when he was interrupted by scribes bringing a woman caught in breaking the law. Notice in verse 6, "But he [Jesus] bent over and wrote on the ground with his finger." A dramatic movement. What do you suppose Jesus wrote in the sand? Why is this included in this Gospel story? It is something to wonder. We do not know. But immediately after this episode Jesus said, "I am the light of the world." Like a light shining upon themselves, the accusers had seen their own guilt and the woman had looked into her darkened past. Perhaps Jesus had used kinesthetic tracing to remember who he was.

Kinesthetic tracing is intriguing to do in moments of boredom or waiting or inactivity. Let these great words of Jesus work themselves deep inside you.

Other phrases of Jesus you can trace and learn are:

> "I am the Bread of Life."
> "I am the Way, the Truth, and the Life."
> "I am the Door."
> "I am the Good Shepherd."

Experience 27: Kinesthetic Tracing for Pre-School Children

1. On the chalkboard write in large letters the word *love*.
2. Children use their index finger as a pointer. The teacher moves their arms and hands to write the word *love*.

3. Children practice alone.
4. Children dip their finger in tempera paint and make the letters of *love* on construction paper.

The teacher says, "God is Love."
Very young children may only be able to make the first letter, L. This is fine. The teacher should tell them, "This means God is Love."

DANCING

If the dance is pleasing, even the lame will crawl to it, is an African saying.

Any discussion of movement in the church must include dance. In almost every land since the first people walked the earth, they have had the urge to dance. Perhaps for the first human beings this language of the whole body came before speech. Perhaps they danced their joys and their sorrows, their successes and their pain.

The primitive way to tell a story is to dance it out. One becomes possessed by the dance and does not dance but "is danced." The simplest, the oldest, and the most powerful of all the arts is beautiful motion.

Dancing is an instinct. Something within us makes us want to dance. This is especially true when we are dealing with feelings. There are certain emotions that are difficult to experience without motion. We dance with joy and are shaken with grief. Dancing may be defined as a way of expressing one's emotions through a rhythmic succession of movements.

In addition to feelings, dance can be a wonderful vehicle for the teaching and articulation of values and beliefs.

Corporate bonds are also strongly forged as persons join together in dance. As we seek to become the body of Christ we wonder, Is it possible to be in touch without touching, to be moved without moving?

Experience 28: Dancing Our Belief About Easter

The Pokot people of East Africa have a dance called "Leap to the Sky." It is an exciting dance to watch. The Pokot tribe are characteristically tall and thin and their long, lean legs are like steel springs. From a flat-footed stance they leap to amazing heights, going higher and higher with the quickening rhythm of the song. They leap on and on tirelessly.

In this experience we borrow from the Pokot tribe of Africa to express our belief about Easter. Using the Easter hymn "Low in the Grave He Lay," follow these instructions:

The class forms a circle with room to move freely between persons. As the words, "Low in the grave he lay, Jesus my savior," are sung, each person sways from side to side in rhythm. The arms hang loose like a pendulum. During the next phrase, "Waiting the coming day, Jesus my Lord," the students continue loosely swaying but bend the body toward the ground. During the Chorus—

Up from the grave he arose,
With a mighty triumph o'er his foes;
He arose a victor from the dark domain,
And he lives forever with his saints to reign.
He arose! He arose! Hallelujah! Christ arose!

Low in the Grave He Lay

—the students stand, hands to their sides, and jump from a flat-footed position on each beat, just a normal jump. On the words "He arose!" they leap high, and on the next "He arose!" they leap higher. On "Hallelujah! Christ arose!" they leap as high as they can. Repeat the same movements on all verses.

Experience 29: Joy to the World

Clement of Alexandria, an early church leader, said, "Then shalt thou dance in a ring together with the angels around Him who is without beginning and end." This experience makes use of the hymn "Joy to the World."

Instructions:
1. The class forms a large circle holding hands.
2. On the first line of the hymn, everyone walks to the center raising clasped hands above their heads as they go.
   (Joy to the world! the Lord is come)
3. Walking backward from the center the class returns to the original wide circle with clasped hands lowered.
   (Let earth receive her King)
4. The circle drops hands. Partners turn and face each other, holding right hands. In grand-right-and-left pattern, students progress around the circle.
   (Let every heart prepare him room)
5. On this line students stop where they are, take both hands of the new partner they now face, and skip around with that partner in a small circle.
   (And heaven and nature sing, And heaven and nature sing)
6. Students drop partner's hands and again become one large circle. On the closing line the large circle walks to the center with hands raised.
   (And heaven, and heaven and nature sing.)

Experience 30: All Things Bright and Beautiful

1. The class stands in a large circle. On the first line of the refrain, they begin a grapevine step to the right. Beginning on the right foot, they cross the left over in front, step with the right and cross the left in the back. Then they repeat this pattern.
   (All things bright and beautiful)
2. Beginning on the left foot, skip in a circle to the left.
   (All creatures great and small)
3. Repeat the grapevine pattern.
   (All things wise and wonderful)
4. Repeat the skipping pattern.
   (The Lord God made them all.)
5. During the singing of the verses of the song, members take turns with each line. One person at a time crosses the length of the large circle in this manner: Take running steps, then let one stride become an elongated leap. Keep the legs straight during the leap. Fling the arms out. End with running steps.

(Each little flower that opens) One student
(Each little bird that sings), one student
(He made their glowing colors), one student
(He made their tiny wings), one student.

6. The entire group dances to the repeated refrain. On succeeding verses different students take solo leaps.

Experience 31: Dance the News

(Youth)

In a class that has had previous experience with movement and dance, try this:
Turn on the radio to a news station. As the students listen to the news they move in whatever way they think appropriate. They may wish to use a finger click, drum beat, or finger cymbals for rhythm. Some movements might include:

> Skipping
> Hopping
> Leaping
> Shaking fists
> Stomping feet
> Jumping
> Rocking on heels
> Reaching up
> Bowing down
> Clogging
> Leapfrogging
> Do-si-doing

MOVEMENT

Bodily movements can be a powerful way of proclaiming the gospel. Following is a service of worship that uses movement and drama to be performed by teenagers for a church community.

Experience 32: Service for Holy Innocents Day

(Youth and Adults)

Holy Innocents Day occurs on December 28. It picks up the story of the murder of the children by Herod after Jesus' birth. Monstrous events, flagrant examples of unjust punishment, are a sad part of human existence. We feel overwhelmed in the face of these atrocities. Something in us fears it could happen again.

The suggested setting for this program is a twilight service in a chapel or sanctuary.

Service for Holy Innocents Day

The leader reads the following from the pulpit:
Sometimes in life we come to a chasm of silence. Ranting and raving do not suffice.

Words fail. Even action is useless. Silence is the only response. Let us enter into an understanding of these deep silences.

There is the silence of great hatred.

(Figure enters carrying a weapon, assumes a hostile pose, feet apart, weapon clutched in fists and held out in front, muscles tight—stage left.)

From a Quaker meeting come these words: Does anyone dare speak here? Speak only if you can improve on the silence. *(Pause)*

There is the silence of great love.

(Woman enters with a baby cradled in her arms. She holds the baby with her head bowed, and stands stage right.)

Does anyone dare speak here? Speak only if you can improve on the silence. *(Pause)*

There is the silence of defeat.

(Figure enters, sits on the floor with knees up, head bowed, one hand on forehead, one hand protecting head—lower stage left.)

Does anyone dare speak here? Speak only if you can improve on the silence. *(Pause)*

There is the silence of deep peace of mind.

(Figure enters, sits cross-legged on the floor, hands on knees, palms up and open, face looking up, eyes shut—lower stage right.)

Does anyone dare speak here? Speak only if you can improve on the silence. *(Pause)*

There is the silence of the unjustly punished.

(Figure enters, stands in slight lunging position, hands above head, crossed at wrist, palms open—center stage.)

Does anyone dare speak here? Speak only if you can improve on the silence. *(Pause)*

There is a silence that is the only response to foolishness that is beyond comprehension. The Bible lifts up two examples.

(Figures leave. Two readers dressed in blue robes enter. One stands at each side of the stage.)

Reader 1:

> The Lord says,
> "A sound is heard in Ramah,
>   the sound of bitter weeping.
> Rachel is crying for her children;
>   they are gone,
>   and she refuses to be comforted.
> Stop your crying and wipe away your tears.
> All that you have done for your children
>   will not go unrewarded;
>   they will return from the enemy's land.
> There is hope for your future;
>   your children will come back home.
> I, the Lord, have spoken."

(Jer. 31:15-17)

(First reader freezes in position after reading.)

Reader 2:

After they had left, an angel of the Lord appeared in a dream to Joseph and said, "Herod will be looking for the child in order to kill him. So get up, take the child and his mother and escape to Egypt, and stay there until I tell you to leave."

Joseph got up, took the child and his mother, and left during the night for Egypt, where he stayed until Herod died. This was done to make come true what the Lord had said through the prophet, "I called my Son out of Egypt."

When Herod realized that the visitors from the East had tricked him, he was furious. He gave orders to kill all the boys in Bethlehem and its neighborhood who were two years old and younger—this was done in accordance with what he had learned from the visitors about the time when the star had appeared.

In this way what the prophet Jeremiah had said came true:
"A sound is heard in Ramah,
    the sound of bitter weeping.
Rachel is crying for her children;
    she refuses to be comforted,
    for they are dead."

(Matt. 2:13-18)

Leader: Today we come together in memory of those babies killed by Herod and we affirm that life is sacred and the future needs to be safe for our children.

There is no argument that favors massive foolishness.

(Two readers leave. Two readers in red robes come on stage.)

Reader 1:   "But he said nothing in response to the accusations of the chief priests and elders.

"So Pilate said to him, 'Don't you hear all these things they accuse you of?'

"But Jesus refused to answer a single word, with the result that the Governor was greatly surprised."

(Matt. 27:12-14)

Reader 2:   "The chief priests were accusing Jesus of many things, so Pilate questioned him again, 'Aren't you going to answer? Listen to all their accusations!'

"Again Jesus refused to say a word, and Pilate was amazed."

(Mark 15:3-5)

Reader 1:   "Herod asked Jesus many questions, but Jesus made no answer."

(Luke 23:9)

Reader 2:   "He was treated harshly, but
        endured it humbly;
    he never said a word."

(Isa. 53:7)

Leader: Special moments stand apart as wordless. Jesus shows us that how a person lives is testimony against which there is no argument. There are times when silence is our most appropriate response.

(Red readers leave.)

Leader: Ancient wisdom from many places tells us there is strength in silence. Hear this Nigerian folktale.

Mother Kite once sent her daughter to find food. She went and brought back a duckling.
(Two actors from the first scene appear.)
Actor 1:   You have done very well my daughter but tell me, what did the mother of this duckling say when you swooped and carried its child away?
Actor 2:   It said nothing; it just walked away.
Actor 1:   You must return the duckling. There is something ominous behind the silence.
Leader: And so Daughter Kite returned the duckling.
(Actors turn away from the audience.)
She took a chick instead.
(Actors turn back and speak.)
Actor 1:   What did the mother of the chick do?
Actor 2:   It cried and raved and cursed me.
Actor 1:   Then we may eat the chick. There is nothing to fear from someone who shouts.
(Actors leave.)

Leader: And finally, when we have kept our silent vigil, when we have stood at the chasm of silence with no words to offer but only our personal testimony, we learn there is healing in silence. Sounds melodious or harsh must all end in silence, yet the silence never dies.

(Choose an appropriate musical selection such as the spiritual, "There Is a Balm in Gilead" and sing it slowly or have a soloist with a timbre of pathos in his or her voice sing it for the class.)

Lord, teach us how to pray. Our peacemaking won't be authentic unless it begins and ends in you.
There's a busy part of us that urges us to be always out doing something.
But you've told us that being quiet with you is essential too.
How can we know what you want us to do if we don't take time out to communicate with you?
Help us not to be afraid of what we might learn if we are still.
Let our lives be a work of peace because we have discovered you and ourselves in you.

Experience 33: Movement Expresses Feelings

(Pre-School)

Begin with the class standing in a circle. Explain that today we are going to experience different ways of walking. First let's try:

1. Bumpy walking
    (Children jump on both feet around circle.)

54

2. Smooth walking
    (Children slide feet as if skating.)
3. Soft walking
    (Children walk on tiptoes.)
4. Strong walking
    (Children march with stamping feet.)
5. Accept other ideas from the class.

Discuss how different ways of walking make you feel different ways. Call on a member of the class to show how we would walk to see baby Jesus in the manger.
   (A child comes to the center of the circle and demonstrates a walk, then others join in.)
Ask someone to show how we would walk if we were little lambs following a good shepherd.
   (A child demonstrates. Others join in.)
Ask another child to show how we would walk if we were in the Palm Sunday parade with Jesus.
   (A child demonstrates. Others join in.)
Walking and moving can express how we are feeling. Ask someone to show by walking how he or she felt on the way to Sunday school this morning.
   (Give each child a chance to express how he or she felt.)
This is a wonderful exercise in creativity and teaches the concept that feelings can be expressed in many ways besides speech.

WORD/SYMBOL

The Word—Introduction

Experience 34: Peter Denies Christ
Experience 35: Jesus Drives Out the Money Changers
Experience 36: Jesus Greets Mary
Experience 37: Rhythm of Words
Experience 38: Jesus' Description of the Pharisees
Experience 39: A Word Game for Easter
Experience 40: You Are the Salt of the Earth
Experience 41: Quality Words
Experience 42: Match Biblical Events with Modern Meanings
Experience 43: Shouts and Cries
Experience 44: The Naming of Things
Experience 45: Personal Names

Symbols—Introduction

Experience 46: Study of the Disciples
Experience 47: Understanding the Bible
Experience 48: Easter Through Symbols
Experience 49: Tour the Sanctuary
Experience 50: Nature Objects
Experience 51: Symbols in Hymns
Experience 52: New Symbols

The language of religion must be that language that relates the human to the infinite, the ultimate to God.

THE WORD—INTRODUCTION

In this section we will be looking at words and symbols as keys to learning about wonder. Surely you say, words involve logic, sequential learning. In many cases they may, but let's look again. A logical use of "scientific" words is instrumental in accomplishing the work necessary for life, but it does not tell us anything about what life feels like in the living.

We often think of the use of words in Sunday school as tools to help us report and express volumes of information. After all, most of our knowledge in Sunday school comes to us orally. But words can also be used to express the feelings of the speaker and that is how we will look at them. Words can convey more than just facts. Words can affect us and shape our beliefs, our prejudices, ideals, aspirations.

Let's look first at three ways words affect us and apply these to Sunday school teaching. The ways are:

1. tone of voice   2. rhythm   3. feelings words evoke.

The following three experiences can be used to supplement and enrich a Lenten or Easter church school session. Their purpose is to make us more sensitive to a biblical incident, to make it come alive for us as we imagine how the words were spoken, and to make us more sensitive to how we speak to others.

We are directly affected by the tone of a voice and its loudness or softness, its pleasantness or unpleasantness.

Experience 34: Peter Denies Christ

(Fourth Grade and Older)

We can understand the story of Peter denying Christ better if we use tone of voice to aid interpretation. Remember learning facts is not our purpose. We seek the feelings behind the words.

1. To prepare for the story read John 13:36-38:

"Where are you going, Lord?" Simon Peter asked him.

"You cannot follow me now where I am going," answered Jesus; "but later you will follow me."

"Lord, why can't I follow you now?" asked Peter. "I am ready to die for you!"

Jesus answered, "Are you really ready to die for me? I am telling you the truth: before the rooster crows you will say three times that you do not know me."

Let different members of the class take turns reading Peter's part. Encourage the students to put themselves in Peter's place and ask themselves what would have been the expression in his voice? What tone?

2. Talk together with your class: Have you ever been accused of something that you were ashamed of? Have you ever lied to deny it? Can you imagine how Peter felt?

3. Have all class members read the following verses to themselves, or read them aloud to the class.

Simon Peter and another disciple followed Jesus. That other disciple was well known to the High Priest, so he went with Jesus into the courtyard of the High Priest's house, while Peter stayed outside by the gate. Then the other disciple went back out, spoke to the girl at the gate, and brought Peter inside. The girl at the gate said to Peter, "Aren't you also one of the disciples of that man?"

"No, I am not," answered Peter.

It was cold, so the servants and guards had built a charcoal fire and were standing around it, warming themselves. So Peter went over and stood with them, warming himself.

(John 18:15-18)

Peter was still standing there keeping himself warm. So the others said to him, "Aren't you also one of the disciples of that man?"

But Peter denied it. "No, I am not," he said.

One of the High Priest's slaves, a relative of the man whose ear Peter had cut off, spoke up. "Didn't I see you with him in the garden?" he asked.

Again Peter said "No"—and at once a rooster crowed.

(John 18:25-27)

4. Talk together: What do you think his tone of voice would have been when Peter first denied knowing Christ? What would have happened to his voice as he continued to be accused and continued to deny it?

5. Now read the story with parts. Choose readers for narrator and three accusers. The remainder of the class reads Peter's replies in unison. Try to make each response more and more agitated.

6. Have members of the class role-play this passage.

7. Instruct students to listen during the week to the tone of voice in which people speak to them. What does the tone of someone's voice tell us about what that person means?

Experience 35: Jesus Drives Out the Money Changers

(Grades 3–6)

Ask the class to read the story of Jesus and the money changers silently, or read it to them yourself.

Jesus went into the Temple and drove out all those who were buying and selling there. He overturned the tables of the moneychangers and the stools of those who sold pigeons, and said to them, "It is written in the Scriptures that God said, 'My Temple will be called a house of prayer.' But you are making it a hideout for thieves!"

(Matt. 21:12-13)

Try reading verse 13 in a variety of ways. Read it sweetly, softly, slowly, loudly, angrily, fast. Ask the class how they think Jesus would have spoken the words.

Discuss the following questions:

— Can a spoken insult be as hurting as a physical blow?

— Some children say they never hit others, but they use cruel insults and harsh words. What is the difference?

— Do you think it is worse to hurt someone physically?

— Are there times when the voice should be raised in anger? when?

This story of Jesus shows us it is all right in some circumstances to say no in anger to an adult.

— If an adult or friend is doing something you know is wrong is it all right to get angry?

— Can you think of some situations where this might apply?

Look at Proverbs 15:1: "A gentle answer quiets anger, but a harsh one stirs it up."

Make a list of words that would stir up anger. Make a list of words that would quiet anger.

Close with prayer: "Gracious God, make us aware of the words we speak. May your presence be heard in our voices and in our speaking."

Experience 36: Jesus Greets Mary

This story of Jesus and Mary takes place immediately after the resurrection of Jesus. Read it together aloud:

Mary stood crying outside the tomb. While she was still crying, she bent over and looked in the tomb and saw two angels there dressed in white, sitting where the body of Jesus had been, one at the head and the other at the feet. "Woman, why are you crying?" they asked her.

She answered, "They have taken my Lord away, and I do not know where they have put him!"

Then she turned around and saw Jesus standing there; but she did not know that it was Jesus. "Woman, why are you crying?" Jesus asked her. "Who is it that you are looking for?"

She thought he was the gardener, so she said to him, "If you took him away, sir, tell me where you have put him, and I will go and get him."

Jesus said to her, "Mary!"

She turned toward him and said in Hebrew, "Rabboni!" (This means "Teacher.")

(John 20:11-16)

Look with the class at verse 16, "Jesus said to her, 'Mary!' " It was the way Jesus said her name that caused Mary to recognize him.

Ask, What do you think Jesus' tone of voice was here?

Experiment with a few different ways of saying "Mary." Some ideas are: soft, gentle, spoken with authority, teasing her for not recognizing him, compassionate, with glad welcome, with rebuke. Which of these do you think best represents the way Jesus felt? why?

This story is a powerful example of how a single word can carry important meaning.

Following this study ask the class members to sit silently and visualize Jesus calling their names. What would be the tone of voice as each of us is addressed? The purpose of this experience is to deepen our commitment to Jesus as we seek to hear his particular call to us. It is to sensitize us to the personal, caring characteristic of Jesus. It is to sensitize in a personal way that calls forth a response of faith.

Note: There is a lesson here for teachers. What tone of voice do you use with your class? It might be interesting to record your voice to detect the message it is delivering. In addition to loudness or softness, pleasantness and unpleasantness, check to see if there is variation in volume and intonation. A continuous tone is boring.

Experience 37: Rhythm of Words

Setting up small rhythmic echoes in one's head is a powerful reinforcement to learning. Rhythm makes it hard to forget.

The following experiences could be a worshipful conclusion to a session studying the healing ministry of Jesus.

EXAMPLE ONE: A LITANY

First ask the class to brainstorm all the examples of healing they recall; for example, cleansing lepers, healing the lame, giving sight to the blind, raising the dead, and so forth.

Set the collected ideas into the blank spaces below in a rhythmic pattern, two healings to a line. Conclude each line with the rhythmic refrain.

_____

Our Lord is a mighty God.
_____

Our Lord is a mighty God.
_____

Our Lord is a mighty God.
_____

The Lord is a mighty God.

EXAMPLE TWO: THE REFRAIN "SAY AMEN"

For this refrain have the class look at Romans 12. Ask each member of the class to read one verse. Then at the conclusion of each verse have the entire class reply "Say amen."

Continue until the entire chapter is read. Your students will hear familiar words in a new way.

EXAMPLE THREE: REPETITION OF A SINGLE WORD

This is a subtle form of rhythm. Look at the beatitudes of Jesus. The word *blessed* reinforces and arouses deeper and more affecting connotations of the words. Have the class read in unison Matthew 5:1-12.

Write beatitudes for your class:

Blessed are the_____

for_____ .

Blessed are the_____

for_____ .

The purpose of these three experiences is to use words in a rhythmic way so as to gather up and summarize. We use affirmation to reinforce commitment.

Experience 38: Jesus' Description of the Pharisees

(Youth)

Words evoke feelings. Sometimes a youth group or church school class will fall into the almost unconscious habit of name-calling or making derogatory remarks about others. This experience might be appropriate for use at such a time.

Read the following story found in Matthew 23:25-28:

How terrible for you, teachers of the Law and Pharisees! You hypocrites! You clean the outside of your cup and plate, while the inside is full of what you have gotten by violence and selfishness. Blind Pharisee! Clean what is inside the cup first, and then the outside will be clean too!

How terrible for you, teachers of the Law and Pharisees! You hypocrites! You are like whitewashed tombs, which look fine on the outside but are full of bones and decaying corpses on the inside. In the same way, on the outside you appear good to everybody, but inside you are full of hypocrisy and sins.

Look closer at Jesus' description of Pharisees: cups dirty on the inside, clean on the outside; whitened tombs. This is not our usual perception of Jesus. Do these words surprise you?

With pencils on a doodle pad, draw the pictures that these words suggest to you: cups, tombstones. What images come to mind? A cartoon style may be used. Share the pictures with the class.

When we are strongly moved we express our feelings by uttering words with affective connotations. Our pictures show how these particular words affect us. Try to imagine the effect these words would have had on the listeners.

Jesus used another device here—direct address. You can almost see him pointing a finger and saying, "And I do mean *you.*" Add a pointed finger to your drawing.

Discuss the following: Often nicknames we give to people evoke feelings. Children can sometimes be very cruel to other children by harassing them and calling them names such as Fatty or Skinny. Any name that makes fun of someone's appearance is cruel. Think how you would feel if it happened to you. Words we use for races and ethnic groups can fall in this same category. Have you had experiences of this at school? Is it ever appropriate to use degrading words?

As Christians we have the obligation to be aware of not just the words we say but the feelings that surround these words. We want to grow as compassionate, caring people.

An intuitive, tactful person is often a person skilled in interpreting tone of voice, facial expressions, and other symptoms of the internal condition of the speaker. Such a person listens not to what is said but how it is said. These three ways, tone of voice, rhythm, and feelings, make up quality of the voice. This quality has a power of expressing feelings that is almost independent of the language used.

Our purpose is to cultivate this intuitive reading of Scripture, which lifts up the internal condition of the speakers, and to relate this to internal conditions we experience in our lives and see in the lives of our students.

Experience 39: A Word Game for Easter

(Fourth Grade and Older)

It is intriguing to think of the power of a word. For example a person may turn pale at the word *rattlesnake* although no snake is present. Words have the power to suggest feelings. This can help us in telling the powerful Easter story.

Provide a large open space in the classroom. Students walk at random through this space. No words are spoken.

The leader joins the meandering group and speaks a word to one person; for example, *quiet*, spoken in a quiet voice. That person speaks the same word to the next person he or she meets.

Those who have received the word must say it to everyone they pass and continue to say it to everyone they meet until everyone is saying the word.

The leader changes the word; for example, to *fear*, spoken in a fearful voice. The same pattern follows, although some will now be saying "quiet" and some "fear." Soon everyone is saying "fear" and the whole mood of the group changes.

Continue the game with words like *run*, *listen*, and so forth.

The teacher says: "Now that we understand how to play the game we will apply it to the Easter story in the Bible."

Directions:

The teacher reads aloud the following verses from Luke 24 while the students meander as in the game above.

"Very early on Sunday morning the women went to the tomb, carrying the spices they had prepared."

(Say the word sad to one member of the group. It travels through the group.)

"They found the stone rolled away from the entrance to the tomb, so they went in; but they did not find the body of the Lord Jesus. They stood there."

(Say the word puzzled. It travels through the group. Some will still be saying "sad.")

"When suddenly two men in bright shining clothes stood by them."

(The leader says fear *and the word travels through the group.)*

"The women bowed down to the ground, as the men said to them, 'Why are you looking among the dead for one who is alive? He is not here; he has been raised.' "

(The leader says the word wonder. *It travels through the group.)*

The leader pauses here until all are saying "wonder." Then he or she continues by saying, "The women went to tell all these things to the disciples."

(The leader says the word joy. *It travels through the group.)*

"But the disciples did not believe them."

(The leader says the word lies. *It travels through the group. Some are still saying joy.)*

"But Peter got up and ran to the tomb."

(The leader says the word run and it travels through the group.)

"He bent down and saw the grave cloths but nothing else. Then he went back home."

(The leader says the word amazed and the word travels through the group.)

Experience 40: You Are the Salt of the Earth

(Elementary Through Adult)

Metaphors are another use of words that is not logical or sequential. A metaphor is a direct comparison. For example, you've heard someone say, "I'm so tired I'm dead." That's nonsense if interpreted literally, but it expresses the feeling of the speaker: I am really tired! Or, if someone is revolted by the conduct of someone else at dinner and has felt the same revulsion watching pigs at a trough, such a person might say, "He is a pig." A simile is similar to a metaphor but it modifies the statement somewhat. You might say, "He is like a pig rather than he is a pig." A simile points out the similarities between the person and the pig. In addition to strongly expressing a feeling, a simile attempts to report a little more accurately. Both figures of speech are used to communicate feelings rather than literal thoughts. Jesus spoke in metaphors and similes.

Give each student a sheet of paper with the word *salt* at the top. See who can list the most words telling what salt does. For example, it makes food taste better.

Have all persons look at their lists and ask themselves, How am I like salt? What or who do I make better by my presence?

Ask the class what they think Jesus meant when he used this metaphor.

Look at the metaphor, "You are the light of the world." Follow the same steps as above. Determine what light does. Think about how each of us is a light to someone else. Share answers. Discuss ideas about what Jesus meant in making this statement.

Another simile to look at is this simile of Jesus: "The kingdom of heaven is like treasure buried in a field" (Matt. 13:44).

Imagine finding a treasure. List all the feelings you would have, for instance, great joy and suspicion? Try to imagine these feelings applying to the Kingdom of heaven. Make comparisons. Discuss the main feeling you think Jesus was trying to capture in this comparison.

The use of metaphors and similes helps us think in images. Comparing one thing to another, unrelated thing gives us new insight into meaning. It is an "ah ha" kind of learning. Jesus constantly pushed his listeners to new ways of thinking, of seeing and interpreting events. Pondering these thoughts of Jesus expressed in metaphors and similes expands our own understanding.

Experience 41: Quality Words

(Youth)

During the Lenten season, take a word as a focal point for your meditation and spiritual growth. Choose a quality word that describes a Christian quality that needs developing in your life, such as:

> patience
> joy
> compassion
> serenity

Write the quality word in the center of a piece of paper. Meditate on this quality word. Let the word guide your thinking. In its many dimensions let it work deep within you.

As you think of other words you associate with the quality word, write these words like spokes to a wheel with the quality word as the hub.

Experience 42: Match Biblical Events with Modern Meanings

(Youth)

Whenever a group of people have memories and traditions in common, extremely subtle and efficient affective communications become possible through the use of allusions. There is a common background of information that is known or is assumed to be known.

In literature, movies, and all forms of communication in the Western world, references are made to biblical events and persons. Meaning is lost if we do not understand these allusions.

In fairly recent years a whole body of literature has arisen from Africa, written, not from the Western point of view about Africa, but from the perspective of the native Africans themselves. The allusions and subtle references they use are to oral stories that are foreign or unknown to Western culture.

With a biblical allusion we can often arouse reverent or pious attitudes. But this works only when the hearer is familiar with the events alluded to. We therefore have a responsibility to teach Bible stories so that our own and our students' understanding will increase. It would be interesting to make a list of Biblical allusions for your Sunday school class. Here is one method to try.

Copy the following "Biblical Allusions" on slips of paper of one color. Copy "Modern Meanings" on slips of paper of another color. Leave off the numbers. Make enough copies so that each pair of students will have a complete set of biblical allusions and modern meanings.

Biblical Allusions	Modern Meanings
1. Judas	1. Someone who betrays
2. Mark of Cain	2. A sign of past evil
3. Cutting Samson's hair	3. Losing your strength
4. When Gabriel blows his horn	4. End of the world
5. Meets his Goliath	5. Experiences a great struggle
6. Scapegoat	6. Someone innocent taking the blame
7. Manna from heaven	7. Taken care of in a crisis
8. Sodom and Gomorrah	8. A place of evil

Have pairs of students match the allusions with their meanings for today. Or, divide the class in half. Give each student in one group one biblical allusion and each student in the other group one modern meaning. Allow several minutes for the students to mingle and find the person who has the slip of paper that matches theirs. When a pair thinks they have a match, they should sit down together and prepare to share with the group why they think their papers match.

Compare answers and discuss the Bible story or incident from which the expression came. Use a Bible dictionary if needed.

Have the students think of other allusions. Assign the class to listen for a week to television and casual conversation. Are there allusions to biblical events or persons? Ask class members to bring in their lists to share with the class.

Experience 43: Shouts and Cries

(Youth and Adults)

Sometimes feelings go beyond words to shouts and cries. Cries expressive of such internal conditions as hunger, fear, loneliness, and triumph may be grunts and gibbering rather than logical statements. For example, if you cut your finger your first response is "ow!" which is an automatic response expressing your feelings. Or, in extreme situations we may gather all our resources into one outcry, "Help!"

Looking at the book of Psalms in the Bible, we read of these cries for help. We will try to experience the depth of feeling in some of these words by shouting a psalm verse.

Divide the class into two groups. Have the groups stand on opposite sides of the room facing each other. Group one will say a line of the psalm given them by the teacher and group two will reply with the following line, antiphonal style. These lines will be repeated five times. Each time the words should become louder, until on the fifth time each group is shouting its line.

Group One: **Group Two:**

(Ps. 17:1)
Listen, O Lord, to my plea for justice.   Pay attention to my cry for help.

(Repeat five times)

Discuss: Where in the world today are people crying out for justice? Can you identify with their feelings?

(Ps. 22:1)
My God, my God, why have you   I have cried desperately for help, but still it
abandoned me?   does not come.

(Repeat five times)

Discuss: You recognize these words from Jesus on the cross. Can shouting these words help you grasp the depth of his anguish a little better?

How could this be used in church school teaching? When or where would it be appropriate? An experience such as this can be inserted in a factual study of peace and justice. Just this brief experience focusing on the feelings can add depth to the study. In so doing, we go beyond learning about something "out there" and identify with the feelings of the persons in the situation.

Experience 44: The Naming of Things

(Elementary to Adult)

To control something is to name it. Perhaps the story of Helen Keller best captures this truth for us. Born blind, deaf, and mute, she did not know things had names. Later on, in one glorious moment as her teacher wrote w-a-t-e-r in the palm of her hand, she made the leap from sensation to symbol. The wonderful, cool something flowing over her hand had a name—water. By knowing the name it could be mentioned, conceived, remembered, controlled. Suddenly the truth dawned on Helen Keller. Everything had a name and each name gave birth to a new thought.

Have you ever had the experience of being temporarily sick and not knowing what was wrong and then going to the doctor and having your illness diagnosed? How great! You are still just as sick but your illness has a *name* and you are reassured it can be controlled. Naming gives us power.

The Bible is full of naming stories. In the beginning Adam names the animals. We end our prayers with the words, "In the *name* of Jesus."

1. Read some of the Bible stories about changing the names—
   a. Abram to Abraham   (Gen. 17:5)
   b. Sarai to Sarah   (Gen. 17:15)
   c. Jacob to Israel   (Gen. 35:10)
   d. Simon to Peter   (John 1:42)
2. Act out these stories.
3. Give yourself a name that is a Christian quality. If you were to put a name on your sweatshirt that expressed a quality you seek in your life, or see the possibility of attaining, what would it be? When Jesus saw Peter he saw in him what no one would have thought was there and named him Rock. Peter eventually changed and became a "rock." What kind of name or names does Jesus find in you?

Experience 45: Personal Names

Before we leave this study of words and their power, here is one more thought. I once read a gripping short story about a person transported to a strange land. He found himself walking down a crowded street where no one addressed him, greeted him, or spoke his name. The story captured the loneliness, actually the horror, of not being addressed, the panic of going nameless up and down streets without salutations. In a nursing home the same week I heard a resident say, "No one is still living who calls me by my first name." The pathos of this statement haunts me.

Each day we can greet a few persons by name. We can salute them at work, in shopping areas, at school, or at home by phone.

We love to hear our name called. We perk up when we hear our name. Our attention is caught if we see our name in print.

A fun thing I like to do with youth is add to their list on Scavenger hunts, "Find a book that has your name or your family's name printed in it." Most cannot figure this out, but one group usually goes and returns triumphantly with a telephone directory.

Recently I had the unsettling experience of entering my home to find a strange, masked man going through my things. After my initial reaction that it was someone playing a joke in a ski mask, I sensed something was very wrong and from deep within me came the question, "Who are you?" My first response to fear was to seek a name. When he did not give me one I screamed and screamed. No name—faceless evil.

This all points to the obvious—the importance of knowing your students names and calling them by name often. Are you ever guilty, as I often am, of calling a student by the name of an older brother or sister you have taught previously? We owe our students the respect of knowing and calling their names.

SYMBOLS—INTRODUCTION

The use of symbols is another powerful form of teaching to wonder. A symbol is something that stands for or points to something else. Our challenge in the church school is to find and use symbols that point to the holy.

Perhaps the most common use of symbols in the church school is the use of an object or picture to remind us of a Bible story and the feelings and concepts this story encompasses.

Perhaps children will not experience the depth of symbols that an adult experiences, but I believe even children can know the rightness of a symbol:

A Cup for Grace
A Manger for Incarnation
A Cross for Sacrifice

In using symbols we are trying to take an intangible abstraction and bring it down to a concrete specific. We can begin with very young children to add the depth of symbol teaching to our Sunday school.

Begin with the symbols of Christmas as you tell the Incarnation story to pre-schoolers.

A Star
A Manger
A Candle
A Shepherd's Crook
An Angel

The first thing we can do with these symbols is to envision the story. Let these picture symbols tell and retell the Christmas story to our young children. Young children can draw these symbols in a number of ways. Actual objects such as a candle, manger, or shepherd's crook can be touched and handled. Representations of angels and stars can also be touched and handled. Then let the children (ages 3 and 4) pick up the objects and tell you the story.

Throughout the Sunday school fill your rooms with the symbols of our faith. Surround our children with them, create them, paint them, construct them, hang them on the walls and the door posts and the bulletin boards, put them on the windows and ceilings.

Here are some suggested symbols for the classrooms that seem appropriate for the ages given:

69

PRE-SCHOOL

Lamb—Jesus the Good Shepherd

Nature symbols—this is my Father's world

Manger at Christmas

Butterflys at Easter

Flower symbols—Easter lily, poinsettia, the rose

Stars

ELEMENTARY

(Since the life of Jesus is often emphasized here, these symbols seem appropriate.)

Symbols of the twelve disciples

Fish

Sacred monograms—IHS, Alpha and Omega

Lamb of God

Different types of crosses and what each means

YOUTH

Torch—symbol of learning

Symbols for God—hand or eye

Symbols for Jesus—fish, Lamb of God, sacred monograms

Symbols for the Holy Spirit—dove, seven flames, triangle

Symbols for the twelve disciples

Symbols for the church—the ship, the ark

Fork in the road—vocation and life choices

Experience 46: Study of the Disciples

(Elementary)

There are symbols for each of the twelve disciples. Sometimes children envision the disciples all lumped together as a crowd around Jesus with Judas and Peter as the only two identifiable. A creation of a shield with a symbol for each disciple will make that disciple personal and serve as a teaching device that lifts up through the symbol an aspect of the Christian faith.

Have each member of the class choose a disciple and read several Bible verses to gain information about that disciple. You could also provide an information sheet about each disciple by making a copy of a page from a Bible dictionary.

There are many books on Christian symbols that give brief descriptions of the disciples as well as details and often pictures of the disciple symbols. Such books serve as excellent models for this study. Look in your church library for *Our Christian Symbols* by Friedrich Rest (New York: Pilgrim Press, 1954) or *Young Readers Book of Christian Symbolism* by Michael Daves (Nashville/New York: Abingdon Press, 1967) as well as any other books on symbols your library might have.

Ask each student to create a shield on cardboard or construction paper.

After reading about his or her disciple, each student creates a disciple shield for him or herself choosing a symbol that reflects something from the life of the disciple. The

PETER   ANDREW   PHILIP   JOHN   JUDE

student should use tempera paint, wide-tip felt pens, or other implements to draw the symbol for the disciple.

Experience 47: Understanding the Bible

(Fourth Grade and Up)

Learning how to read the Bible is not easy. Its stories were written two thousand and more years ago. The Bible is like no other book ever written. It is the Word of God in the past and, in some mysterious way, the Word of God for our lives today. It is historical but it is beyond history. It is factual but it is beyond facts. The Bible is something that confronts us.

Perhaps symbols can come to our rescue as we attempt to help our students understand the Bible. As we study, create, and then contemplate some traditional symbols for the Bible we will begin to discern its deeper meaning.

The symbol of the Bible as a lamp is a traditional one. The lamp pictured is usually the ancient oil-burning lamp with its graceful shape and tiny flame, which sends out ever-increasing circles of light. Find a picture of this symbol and display it for your class.

Have the class read and memorize Psalm 119:105, "Your word is a lamp to guide me and a light for my path."

List all the words you associate with lamp. Encourage the children to speak when they are ready. Assure them that all answers are acceptable. The class here is supposed to devise a long list of imaginative and practical uses of lamps. Give the imaginations free range.

Shift the focus just a bit by asking this question: What if we just take the flame? Have the class offer all the uses of a flame they can think of. See if the class comes up, from either of these questions, with suggestions related to intelligence, learning, wisdom, or knowledge. See if the concept surfaces of past, present, and future.

Using the ideas given by the class, circle the ones that best answer, How is the Bible like a lamp?

Create a class banner using the lamp as a symbol.

Experience 48: Easter Through Symbols

(Grades Three and Four)

The Easter message is difficult to teach children. Again symbols can come to our aid. They indicate pictorially the cardinal elements of Easter.

Step 1: Display these symbols before the class:

          palm branch
          chalice and wafer
          purse and thirty pieces of silver

cock crowing
cross
butterfly

Step 2: Students each choose one symbol and write a paragraph about it. This may be a biblical story they know, an Easter legend they have heard, or an original story.

Step 3: Share the stories. Identify the biblical background of the first five symbols if they are not known, and explain why the life cycle of the butterfly is a symbol of Easter if this is not known.

Step 4: Create the symbols for an Easter transparent mobile for your room using the following directions:

    a. Cut large shapes of the symbols from black construction paper. Cut out two identical shapes for each symbol.

    b. Cut large holes in each shape so that there are spots big enough to see through.

    c. Cut pieces of colored cellophane large enough to cover the holes.

    d. Staple the cellophane between the two pieces of black paper you have cut for each shape.

    e. Punch a hole in the top and attach yarn or string.

    f. Hang with string or yarn from the ceiling of your classroom. (The butterfly symbols when finished look particularly nice.)

Experience 49: Tour the Sanctuary

(Pre-School and Up)

Take your class on a tour of your sanctuary looking for symbols. Your minister or someone from the worship committee of your church might lead this tour.

Sometimes the shape of the church itself may be a symbol; for example, churches built in the shape of a cross. Sometimes a lectern contains the symbols of an eagle or a pelican. Find out why. Some churches have windows filled with symbols. The baptistery, the altar area, and sometimes even the pews are decorated with symbols. If your sanctuary is particularly rich in symbolism it could be fun for elementary children to go on a treasure hunt specifically designed for your sanctuary. There are two values in studying your individual church symbols: devotional and educational. The central ideas of Christianity can be approached through your particular church symbols.

The use of symbols in the examples above depends on knowing the biblical story. The relationship of the symbol to the story is crucial. This use of symbols seeks to add depth to the story and to remind us of the feelings the story conveys. The symbol is representative of what is being studied.

Symbols can become something through which the holy is manifested or made present. This most powerful use of symbols usually occurs during worship in the sanctuary. We partake of the sacraments and feel God present with us.

How wonderful it would be if we could capture something of this divine Presence in our classrooms and our classes could become laboratories of wonder.

Holiness is present in everything. Nature gives us a gateway or opening to this sense of wonder. Why not have a wonder table for all ages in the church school? Recall the suggestions for wonder we made at the beginning of this book under "Classroom Climate" (butterfly wings and seashells and delicate snowflakes). Perhaps these objects can begin to point beyond themselves to the sacred. Perhaps they can become openings where the holy can enter the world.

Beware of anything that takes wonder out of a child. We are closing doors to worship. Instead we must work to see the holy present in our ordinary world. Look for miracles and manifestations in our very midst. Whenever you see or experience anything of great beauty, truth, goodness, help your children see that the source is God. God can break through into the ordinary—even our classrooms.

Experience 50: Nature Objects

(Youth and Older)

Take an object from nature and let it become a symbol for you.
Read and memorize Psalm 1:3:

> They are like trees that grow beside a stream,
>   that bear fruit at the right time,
>   and whose leaves do not dry up.
> They succeed in everything they do.

Complete this sentence: If I were a tree I would be a _____ tree because _____.
Share your answers.
Assume a position of meditation. Listen to this legend from the Eastern world:

> There was once a young man who wished to learn about God. He asked everyone he knew to tell him about God and still he wasn't satisfied. So he went to nature.
> After many unsuccessful attempts he came to the almond tree. "Speak to me of God," he begged. The almond tree blossomed and he understood.

(The teacher continues to speak with periods of silence between sentences.)
Throughout history trees have held religious symbolism for humans.
As you think about the tree you have chosen for your symbol consider each stage of its growth.
Think about smallness and roots—both the tree's and yours.
Think about growth and risk taking—both the tree's and yours.
Think about change.
Think about fruit or blossoms.
Think about leaves falling and bare branches and the elderly stage of your life.
Finally, think about God's gift of life that is in both the tree and in you.

This experience might be inserted into a camp setting when the seasons are changing and we are more acutely aware of nature. The purpose is to feel joy and wonder in response to the natural world. We are trying through nature to bring to our consciousness the Creator God.

Experience 51: Symbols in Hymns

(Adult)

Hymns can be a study of symbols for an adult class. The purpose of this experience is to bring new meaning and insight to a traditional symbol.

Share this definition with the class: A symbol is something that stands for, represents, or denotes something else—not by exact resemblance but by vague suggestion.

Have the class choose a favorite hymn and sing it. As an example here let's use "Have Thine Own Way, Lord."

Members of the class should identify all the symbols, for example, "potter" and "clay." Connect a concept with each symbol. For example: Potter—God; clay—Obedience.

Discuss the symbols and concepts. The study may be repeated with other hymns.

Experience 52: New Symbols

We need new symbols for a new age. The problem with selecting new symbols is that they must be right. There is something intrinsic in a symbol.

The newest symbol I see emerging in the church school that seems right to me is the folded paper crane, which symbolizes peace.

The idea of world unity, brotherhood and sisterhood of humans, and world peace seems to be crying for a symbol in our age.

Read to your class the story *Sadako and the Thousand Paper Cranes* by Eleanor Coerr (Dell Yearling Books, P. O. Box 3000, Pine Brook, NJ 07058). This is the beautiful story of a little girl who fell victim to leukemia as a result of the dropping of the atomic bomb during World War II. During her long illness she made paper cranes, because of an old legend that with a thousand cranes a person is healed.

Using origami paper, follow the instructions on the next page to create the cranes.

Remember that we cannot create a new symbol but we can filter one out of an event. Symbols must speak to us with power.

The best symbols are participatory. They help us identify with the experience and they pick up a story. When something does not have or has lost that participative quality, it is no longer a symbol for us.

Balloons are being used a lot as symbols. I have mixed feelings about balloons as symbols in church and Sunday school. In the first place I believe we are overusing them. Balloons are released on numerous occasions with numerous messages and are displayed in the sanctuary during several church seasons and occasions. Beyond realizing that they are harmful to wildlife when ingested, we may ask, What story do they illustrate? No story comes to my mind, either biblical or current.

If, on the other hand, we are using balloons to symbolize a feeling, "celebrate" is certainly a buoyant feeling, a lifting feeling, a feeling of joy akin to praise and confidence, a feeling of hope and possibility. Balloons could symbolize this feeling.

The final criterion is: Does the symbol speak to you with power? And most important, does it point beyond itself to the sacred? I leave the decision about balloons up to you.

We will always need new symbols to express our faith and the time in which we live. Respect for traditional symbols should not keep us from a reverent use of imagination and sensitivity in creating new ones. But the ability is intrinsic. We do not choose a season or Bible story and then give it a twist by inserting devices and techniques and new symbols here and there like acupuncture needles. In a true symbol there is something unmanageable about the way it is formed. It surfaces rather than being created.

Make Origami Cranes

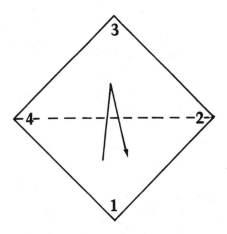

1. Start with a square piece of paper. Turn the paper so it looks like a diamond. Number the corners 1, 2, 3, 4. Fold the paper in half from corner 3 to corner 1.

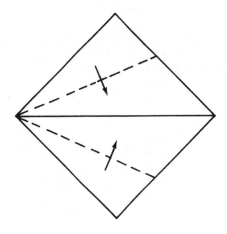

2. Unfold the paper. Fold edge 3-4 to the center crease. Fold edge 4-1 to the center crease.

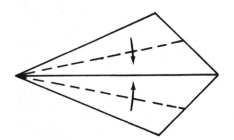

3. Turn the paper over. Fold edges 4-3 and 4-1 to the center crease.

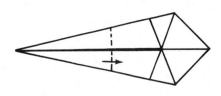

4. The narrow pointed end is the crane's head. The wider pointed end is the tail. Fold the head to the tail.

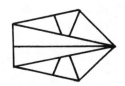

5. Fold the head back about two inches from the point.

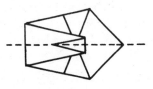

6. Pick the crane up and fold in half downward, lengthwise.

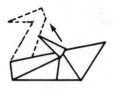

7. Hold at point indicated by black spot on diagram and pull head up. Pinch the back of the head to make a new fold.

8. Hold at point indicated by black spot and pull the neck up. Pinch at the base of the neck to make a new fold.

Origami Crane

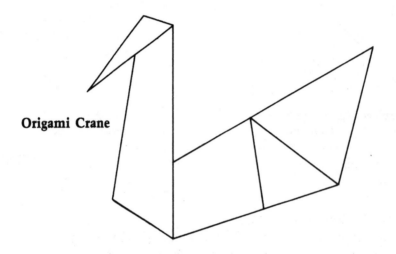

PART IV   ANTITHESIS/PARADOX

ANTITHESIS/PARADOX

Introduction

Paradoxical Language Speaks of the Holy
    Experience 53: Unchanging yet All Changing
    Experience 54: Absorbing Contradictions
    Experience 55: God's Presence
    Experience 56: Jump the Attributes of God

Opposites
    Experience 57: Looking at Hot and Cold
    Experience 58: Making Faces
    Experience 59: Feelings

Experiences for Elementary Children and Youth
    Experience 60: Look at Sin
    Experience 61: Prophets' Words
    Experience 62: Emmaus Walk
    Experience 63: War and Peace

Evil in the World
    Experience 64: Evil—Recognize It
    Experience 65: Evil—Fight It
    Experience 66: Evil—Defeat It

ANTITHESIS/PARADOX

To be human is to be a creature caught in the tension of opposites.

Introduction

As we seek to lead our children to an experience with God, and attempt to teach our children about God, we come across statements, concepts, and beliefs that seem to be contradictions. They seem to be intellectually absurd. For example, there is the Christian concept of Christ as being both fully human and at the same time fully divine. Or, Christ's statement, "The first shall be last." How can we keep such apparently contradictory statements from becoming stumbling blocks for our students?

In this section we attempt to deal with these paradoxical statements and counterbalancing ideas. First we look at paradoxical language as a way of speaking about the holy. Then we look at contradictory experiences from our lives that point to a completeness, a wholeness in our life journey. Finally we look at the problem of good and evil.

As in the previous chapters we try to experience these concepts with our students in some participatory way.

The words from the anonymous writer of the spiritual classic *Cloud of Unknowing* guide us: "Reason cannot fully know God for God cannot be thought, possessed and discovered by the mind. But loved God may be and chosen by the artless, affectionate longing of your heart."

PARADOXICAL LANGUAGE SPEAKS OF THE HOLY

If we go far into the study of seeking to know God we meet with the paradoxes of our faith. Perhaps no one has lifted it up for us as clearly as Augustine in his *Confessions:*

"What art Thou then my God?" he cried, and he enumerates for us vexing problems for our minds to grasp. Among them, these descriptions of God:

unchanging, yet all changing
never old, never new
ever working, ever at rest
still gathering but nothing lacking
seeking yet having all things
most hidden, yet most present

And our minds, though they cannot grasp the logic, affirm the truth of these words. Jesus also spoke to us in this way:

The first shall be last.
He who would be great must be your servant.
He who would save his life must lose it.
I depart and lo I am with you.
My burden is easy. My yoke is light.

Paradoxical language such as that used in these examples is a use of words in a distinctive way. Contradictions are brought together to express a profound truth. Words that if logic was intended, seem negating and absurd, when used to speak of the holy express truth. The sacred is always beyond the power of speech and in groping to express these concepts language is forced beyond its ordinary use.

Conjoining opposites and using paradox are ways of speaking of the ultimate. We use logical, scientific words to refer to the natural world, but what we seek to describe in our search for God is another thing.

Experience 53: Unchanging yet All Changing

(Older Elementary and Youth)

To experience this concept with your class have everyone repeat aloud Augustine's statement "unchanging, yet all changing" several times.

Give each student a sheet of paper with a line down the middle. On one side of the paper, list three characteristics of your personality that have remained unchanged since birth. On the other side, list three ways you have changed in the last five years. Share answers. You are unchanging, yet ever changing.

Now attempt to do this experience with God. This may be harder for your students. On one side of the paper, list all the ways God is unchanging. On the other side, list all the ways God is all changing. Compare answers. Point out how both concepts, though opposite, are true.

In seeking to grasp an understanding of God, we stretch our minds. We seek to develop a feel for a different way of speaking about God. Put aside a way of speaking that seeks to prove through rational approaches. Let paradoxical words speak to you as art does. In a unique way let paradoxical words show you what God is like.

Experience 54: Absorbing Contradictions

Let me try to describe this way of paradoxically speaking of God: Have you ever tried to think of a name long forgotten? You think hard and the name does not come. You go ahead and do other things and the name appears like a light behind your eyes. It is the same with thinking of God in paradoxical terms. If we try to think logically and make sense it eludes us. If we relax, the truth of the statement becomes apparent to us.

For this reason it seems that the best way to "learn" is to memorize, to absorb the words. Take the paradoxical sayings of Jesus such as "The first shall be last" and repeat them over and over to yourself. Let the words work deep within you. Do not try to analyze. And then the meaning will come to you.

A still better way to absorb these words is to set them to music. Take the refrain of a familiar hymn. For example, the refrain of "I Need Thee Every Hour" works well with the words "The first shall be the last" repeated over and over. The hymn "God Be with You Till We Meet Again" works with the words "He who would save his life must lose it." Sing thoughtfully, prayerfully. The refrain to the Fanny Crosby hymn "Jesus, Keep Me Near the Cross" works with the words, "My burden is easy. My yoke is light."

Experience 55: God's Presence

(Youth and Older)

This experience is for a class or group that has had some practice in meditation. It might conclude a retreat or spiritual growth study. It might be used in conjunction with a mission project as participants are returning home.

In this experience we look at two similar paradoxes: God is hidden yet present, and Jesus' words, "I depart and lo I am with you."

In teaching this paradox we will try to capture and create the feelings evoked by the paradox. We will create the feeling and let the mind draw its conclusions. We will attempt to experience these contradictory words in this manner:

1. Sit quietly with your hands in your lap, palms up.
2. Breathe in and out slowly.
3. Say over and over to yourself: "I will be with you always, to the end of the age" (Matt. 28:20). Say the words to the rhythm of your breathing. Relish the words. Repetition channels the mind, thus ingraining habits of thought.
4. Now concentrate on the feel of your hand. Be aware of every sensation. Bring all your attention to this one portion of your body. At first there may be no sensations, but after a time there begins a pricking, a throbbing. Attend in thought to these feelings no matter how faint.
5. You will, after a time, feel a warmth in your palm, God intensely near you. Feel the touch.

Experience 56: Jump the Attributes of God

Since God is above and beyond our limited world, we seek new and different ways of speaking about God. But the idea that God is unknowable brings us to another paradox.

The God who is abstract, infinite, and the object of theoretical reflection is also the God who is personal, knowable, and indwelling nearness. How can we experience the concept that God is both transcendent and immanent?

Have the group stand and in unison jump words that describe the transcendence of God. Each person jumps on both feet for each consonant and hops on one foot for each vowel. For example, "holy" would be jump-hop-jump-jump.

Jump these words, which describe the transcendence of God:

> Infinite
> Eternal
> All-Powerful
> All-Knowing
> Holy
> Awesome
> Sacred
> Mysterious

Jump these words, which describe the immanence of God, God present with us:

> Loving
> Merciful
> Good
> Compassionate
> Just
> Kind
> Patient
> Gentle
> With us

Take a few moments to wonder. Sit quietly and catch your breath. Let your mind dwell on these thoughts: God is always with us, within us, and seeking us. This same God is holy, mysterious, beyond our grasp. How great is our God! The Creator of the universe answers to our cry of "Daddy" or "Mother." Think on these things (reflection after a time of exertion and activity often brings insight).

OPPOSITES

As well as looking at paradoxical statements in the Bible we know experiences of opposites in our own lives. Our own human pilgrimage confirms the paradoxes of life. We are creatures of joy and hurt, pain and ecstasy, despair and hope. We call it antithesis; all those strongly opposed notions placed together or even laid side by side so that we feel the contrast and are stirred by it. Antithesis recognizes the pull and push in all things, the pull and push forces that play with one another, back and forth.

This is a type of learning that cannot be rationally explained so forcefully as it can be experienced. What are we attempting to teach through antithesis? It seems that God is pointing us to a wholeness, a completeness for our lives. Wholeness is marked by polarities. The understanding of wholeness is seen through antithesis. To understand life we must understand the balances. One causes us to see the other, just as we see light against darkness.

We want to teach that life is not static. It has rhythms, cycles, and stages. In nature we see day and night, and the month-by-month waxing and waning of the moon. The cycles of the year—summer, winter, spring, and fall—are mighty orbs of time folding and refolding on themselves. All of human life has these cycles and stages too: life and death, work and rest, joy and sorrow, illness and health, loss and recovery. This we believe is God's plan.

We want to teach that wholeness is inclusive. It includes our suffering and pain as well as our health and comfort. We need to believe and act on the belief that we are participating in God's wholeness. For example, we do not teach that God wants us to be miserable. Quite to the contrary, we teach that in adversity or success we have God's blessing. We move toward an acceptance of everything that is.

The world is filled with positive and negative energy. We all share both types of emotion. Harmony exists at all levels, cellular to universal, when opposites integrate and balance each other. Negative and positive emotions both are important. Both are different aspects of life energy. Expressing but one of either extreme of the polarity misses the mark.

Antithesis reminds us we are not teaching students to be perfectly happy, psychologically perfect, fully healthy spiritually, and to have no doubts. No! Such training would make of them robots. We are teaching students to be fully alive wherever they are, and to know they are under the lordship of God wherever they are. We are teaching them to walk through the valley of shadows as well as beside still waters. We are teaching them to be completely painted with shadows and shades, with wrinkles and lines, with scars and wounds, visible and invisible. We seek to be the creatures God meant us to be, partaking in all of life.

Can a life that has not known the depths reach to the heights? We believe that if we close ourselves to pain, our capacity for pleasure also dies. A hothouse flower, without insect nibbles on its leaves, with blossoms ruler straight, is not so beautiful to me as a stunted blossom that has fought its way to the sun through molded leaves and animal trampling. The color seems more vivid, the fragrance more delicate.

I feel the same about animals in the zoo. A lion in a zoo cannot be compared to a lion seen on an African safari. When I saw one in the wild I felt that I had never really seen a lion before. The animal, caged and protected, was but a shadow of the magnificent creature living free on the savanna, facing life's uncertainties daily.

Is this true of humans? Have we sheltered our lives, hiding from death, pestilence, and sickness? Have we hidden from anything that is too hard or too uncomfortable until we are sickly creatures? Are we poor imitations of what we are meant to be?

Our faith speaks to us here of perspective and fullness of life. Only by facing our potential for good and for bad do we see wholeness, perspective, and balance for an integrated life.

These are lofty concepts that may seem too impractical and illogical to teach. How do we teach that our children may understand? In the following experiences we seek to acquaint our young children with the world of opposites in conditions and feelings. With elementary children and youth the experiences seek to illustrate opposites they are now experiencing. Finally we will look at that ever-challenging antithesis, good versus evil. We will seek to experience our faith's affirmations.

The following three experiences can be used in your regular church school setting as a way to enrich your session. Plan to use these experiences in conjunction with your curriculum. Use them as a way to expand a Bible story or verse.

Experience 57: Looking at Hot and Cold

In the pre-school years we want our children to become aware of opposites. Temperature is a good place to begin.

Idea 1: Fill three small tubs with water: one hot, one cold, one warm. Let the children take turns feeling the difference.

Idea 2: Play the game Hot or Cold. The teacher says a word or phrase and the class replies "hot" or "cold." Words to begin with *(add your own):*

> fireplace
> oven
> refrigerator
> sun
> ice
> under a quilt
> in a swimming pool
> snowman
> dryer

Idea 3: Acting it out. Ask, Who in the class can show us how it feels to be hot? Who can show us how it feels to be cold? Now let's all make believe we are playing in the snow *(the class acts out).* Now let's pretend we are barefoot on a hot sandy beach *(the class acts out).*
(If snow or the beach has not been experienced by your children choose similar experiences that relate to your locale.)

Idea 4: Guessing hot or cold. Children stand facing the wall, eyes shut, hands behind them. The teacher quickly touches the palm of a child's hand with an object. The child responds "hot" or "cold." *(An ice cube and a piece of fur are good objects to use. For safety we choose fur although the object is warm, not hot. In contrast to an ice cube, it will be distinguishable.)*

Tell the children that God made "hot" things for us to enjoy and "cold" things for us to enjoy. Our world is more interesting and exciting because we have both.

This is a good game to play with "hard" and "soft" and "sharp" and "smooth." You may think of other opposites to add.

Experience 58: Making Faces

Another way to prepare young children for understanding antithesis is by helping them make faces to express various emotions. This helps develop their sensitivity and empathetic capacities.

Bring a hand mirror into your classroom. Instruct your children to make:

1. a happy face.
2. a sad face
3. a mad face
4. a surprised face
5. a disgusted "icky" face
6. a silly face

Let the children look in the mirror and see their expressions.

Help the children understand that many different ways of feeling are inside us and these feelings show on our faces. We all have these different feelings at times.

With four and five-year-olds, you can read a Bible story and let the class make the appropriate face. Look at your Sunday school curriculum material and see if you can use one of the suggested stories in this manner. Here is an example that is appropriate for older elementary children.

The Good Samaritan

One day a man started to travel from Jerusalem to Jericho. As he went along the lonely road he met some robbers.
(Make robbers' face—mad.)
They took his money, beat him up, and left him.
(Make the face of the wounded man—sad.)
Presently a priest came down the road and he saw the poor man lying there. But he didn't stop.
(Make a stuck-up face.)
After the priest, a Levite came. When he saw the poor man he was disgusted and hurried on.
(Make an icky face.)
The man would have died but a kind-hearted Samaritan came along. He looked at the man with pity.
(Make a loving face.)
He stopped and bound up the beaten man's wounds. Then he gave him a drink to revive him.
(The wounded man makes a smiling face.)
Because of the Good Samaritan the man lived.

With exaggerated facial expressions the children can dramatize emotions of the various characters.

Experience 59: Feelings

(Elementary)

Another way to illustrate your curriculum material that deals with feelings is the following.

Give each child a white paper plate and crayons. Instruct the children to draw opposite faces on each side of the plate, an angry face on one side and a loving face on the other. The children then share their faces. Then they turn them back and forth at appropriate times during a story.

The story of Mark 10:13-16, where Jesus blesses the little children, is appropriate here.

Some people brought children to Jesus for him to place his hands on them,
  (smiling faces)
but the disciples scolded the people.
  (frowning faces)
When Jesus noticed this, he was angry and said to his disciples, "Let the children come to me, and do not stop them, because the Kingdom of God belongs to such as these. I assure you that whoever does not receive the Kingdom of God like a child will never enter it."
  (frowning faces)
Then he took the children in his arms, placed his hands on each of them, and blessed them.
  (smiling faces)

Following the story, punch a hole in the top of the plate and hang the plates by string or yarn from the ceiling. Remind the children that we all share the feelings of both anger and love in our lives. We have other opposite feelings inside us too.

Play a game of opposites. Tell the children that when you suggest a feeling they are to tell you the opposite feeling. For instance:

> happy—sad
> afraid—fearless
> laugh—cry
> worry—trust
> weak—strong
> sick—well
> quiet—loud

Pray with the children: Teach us, O God, how we may be awake to our living experience and how we may make our students more aware. We offer you our pain and our joy, our weakness and our strength, all that we are, to be used by you.

Amen.

A whole person has all these feelings inside. Wisdom is being able to know the appropriate moment to express each of these feelings. Our best guideline is to look at the life of Jesus.

EXPERIENCES FOR ELEMENTARY CHILDREN AND YOUTH

Experience 60: Look at Sin

The classic Christian experience is the coming together of opposites—God's love and human sin. On the one hand are human beings—sinful, full of pride and selfishness. On the other hand is God, whose goodness is so profound God's Son, Jesus, died for us. Reconciliation between the two is possible and indeed has already been accomplished.

In our educational program the church must take into account plain old sin. We have tended to shrink from this massive concept. We tend either to ignore the doctrine of sin or limit it to things like "Put away your toys" or "Don't use bad language."

The following may help children understand.

Go outside to a seesaw. Say to the children "None of us is so good as he or she would like to be. All of us do things that are wrong." Choose three children. Hang a sign around the neck of each child. Each sign has one word: "Pride," "Selfishness," and "Meanness."

Tell the children "These three children will represent all of us human beings that are not so good as we would like to be. You three sit on one side of the seesaw."

"Now, on the other side is God, who is always good and loving." Choose three children of the approximate size of the other three. They are to sit on the opposite side of the seesaw. They seesaw back and forth.

"This is like life. Here is sinful humanity forgetting and denying God, and here is the loving God who forgives us and takes us back. All through the Old Testament this same story is repeated over and over."

"But God did one thing that really tipped the balance. He loved us so much he sent his Son to die for us." Two more children represent Jesus and get on God's side of the seesaw.

"This tips the balance in God's favor doesn't it?"

We are attempting here to experience this concept rather than just explain it. Perception into reality, which is the principal task of study, takes place not only verbally and logically. We learn through our experiences.

This experience can be used during your regular Sunday school class if you have easy access to a seesaw. The Lenten season of the year is a good time to use it.

Experience 61: Prophets' Words

A study of the prophets occurs periodically in church curricula. The study of the Prophets in the Old Testament casts an interesting light on perspectives. During times of pain for the nation of Israel, their message was comfort and hope. During times of plenty, their message was warning of doom. The following experience can be used in conjunction with such a study.

Directions:

Have the students look through recent newspapers for examples of pain and problems in the world and cut them out. Ask, What word of hope could be given in reply to these articles? For example, what word of hope is there for the people in South Africa? Is there a Christian word? The word *gospel* means "Good News." What good news can you give here?

Have the class look through newspapers for examples of plenty and abundant wealth in the world and cut them out. Then ask, What word of doom would you give in reply to these articles? For example, what word to the life-style of the rich and famous? Is there a Christian word? What would the prophets of the Old Testaments have said?

You may wish to share here the story of the Wall of Jerusalem. The Wall in the very center of the city is the place where Jews come to pray. Bar Mitzvahs are held here. The Wall is a boundary line between the Jewish and the Arab sections of the city. It is a broken wall. Instead of repairing it, the Jews decided to leave it as it is so that those who see the Wall ask, What must be done to repair and rebuild the world? It is broken to suggest wholeness. Remembering pain is a way of affirming hope.

The same idea is picked up in a Jewish wedding where traditionally there is the breaking of a glass. It is a happy time, but a moment set aside to remember pain adds perspective.

Forgetting is the sacrilege. "May I never be able to play the harp again if I forget you, Jerusalem" (Ps. 137:5).

Perspective and balance make for wholeness in life.

Experience 62: Emmaus Walk

This is a project for a summer camp experience. Set up a walking course over a large outdoor area. Students follow the trail and walk as directed at each stop:

1. Walk on a trampoline (or jump).
2. Cover trampoline with balls (students must walk through these).
3. Walk a plank.
4. Walk a tightrope.
5. Hop through a tire obstacle course.
6. Walk through water.
7. Walk over rough stones.
8. Walk through grass, barefooted.
9. Walk through mud.

Work out other walks as suits your terrain. Just make sure there are a variety of walks; some easy and pleasant, some difficult. After the group has completed the walks they sit on the grass as the leader reads:

> On that same day two of Jesus' followers were going to a village named Emmaus, about seven miles from Jerusalem, and they were talking to each other about all the things that had happened. As they talked and discussed, Jesus himself drew near and walked along with them; they saw him, but somehow did not recognize him.
>
> (Luke 24:13-16)

The leader then says, "Your life is like the walk you just took. Some places are hard, some places easy. Jesus is walking along with you just as he did at Emmaus. We had to change the way we walked to get through some of the places. In our lives we will have to make changes and adjust, but remember that God is unchangeable and at the same time God changes to meet our circumstances and be with us."

Experience 63: War and Peace

Make a war-and-peace scrapbook. Purchase a large scrapbook. Have the children look through current magazines for pictures of war, conflict, and arguments. Also look for pictures of peace, community, and brotherhood. Cut the pictures out.

Paste all pictures of war, collage-style, on one side of the page. Opposite, on the facing page, paste all pictures of peace, collage-style.

Continue this activity until the scrapbook is full. This is a good project for those "times between the cracks." We all have them in our church school teaching. For some lessons we want to begin all together and creating the war-and-peace scrapbook is a good project for early arrivers. On some Sundays we end early. The bell hasn't rung but our lesson has reached its conclusion. This is another good time for the scrapbook project. Sometimes right in the middle of a lesson some students may finish an assignment early and you don't wish to rush the rest of the class. Let these children work on the scrapbook. It should be a continuing project that doesn't become dated.

EVIL IN THE WORLD

The great mystery, the great unknown in Christianity, is also a paradox: Good versus Evil.

This raises so many questions for us: Why is there evil in the world? If God is all powerful and also all good, how can we account for evil? Is evil something within ourselves? Is it another god? or is evil the dark side of God?

I (and I am assuming that many of you are like me) do not have a clear-cut answer in my own mind. Evil is a mystery. Yet I feel we must not avoid facing this issue with our students. We should enter into the mystery together.

We can make three affirmations about good and evil and try to experience these truths. These affirmation from our heritage are: Evil is a reality, we fight against it, and love has conquered evil.

Experience 64: Evil—Recognize It

First we come to terms with the pervasive fact of evil. Our historical faith tells a story. It is a wonderful, symbolic story that we can try to experience. It is possible to use this experience in a class without previous experience in meditation but it will be more effective with a class that has had such experiences.

Tell class members to close their eyes and get comfortable. Then speak slowly the following to the class, taking plenty of time so the students can see and feel:

Take a few deep breaths. Now think of the most beautiful garden you can possibly imagine. Let your imagination populate it with gorgeous flowers and trees. Imagine fabulous colors and aromas and patterns. Walk in it and among it. Add vegetables and grasses to your scene. Feel complete happiness and peace and contentment. This is your home. A warm sun shines upon this place making it glisten and sparkle. The garden home is bounded on all sides by four rivers. Imagine the beauty of these rivers. Each one is a little different from the others. Look at the shade or hue of colors: translucence, blue, green, aqua, foam. See the rivers as still and deep. Stay with this image until you feel peace.

Now imagine a snake appearing directly in the path in front of you in this garden-home.

Get in touch with your feelings of repulsion, yet fascination. Experience the desire to run and yet come closer. Feel yourself being drawn closer and closer. You have seen birds hypnotized by snakes. You feel yourself under the same power. You feel repulsion and fascination.

Holding you with its hooded eyes, swaying slightly from side to side, the snake asks you to do something. You want to run but a power comes out of the snake that stops you. Mechanically, like a robot, you respond to the serpent's request. You bite into a crisp, juicy forbidden fruit and then pass it on to another.

Suddenly the peace is gone from you. The great serenity you experienced has vanished and so has the snake. The garden home is gone.

You are left puzzled and shattered. The pull to know again that great peace and beauty is there and yet the knowledge that it is somehow lost possesses you.

You turn and begin to walk down a long, dusty path not really sure where you are going. When you are ready, open your eyes.

This ancient story from our heritage confirms that there is evil in the world. The story confirms that it is the human experience to know it. It confirms that evil has tremendous power and pull. Evil separates us from the love of God. Evil is somehow the opposite of all that we know as light and good and affirming and healing throughout God's creation.

To understand wholeness of life we recognize that evil is a universal reality. It has a deep malignant nature so terrifying to us we seldom face it in ourselves and others. We live, within ourselves, within our world, and within the cosmos, with the antithesis of good and evil.

Experience 65: Evil—Fight It

Try this experience with your youth group. In addition to helping our students accept and face the reality of evil in the world, we can share another historical position we take in regard to evil. We fight it! The Christian position is not to passively accept this evil as a necessary part of our existence but to battle with evil. Evil is something to do battle with!

The United Methodist Church decided recently to revise its hymnal. A committee doing very thorough and extensive work looked into this task.

One suggestion that arose was that the hymn "Onward, Christian Soldiers" be eliminated from the new edition, because of the connotation of war and destruction.

From the grass roots of the church, a great cry of opposition arose. It even made the national magazines and newscasts. The nerve that this was hitting, it seems to me, is the basic feeling we have that evil is something we battle against. The hymn was expressing feelings, not about war between individuals and nations, but about cosmic war with the powerful forces of evil.

Sing with your class the hymn "Onward, Christian Soldiers" and the great Martin Luther hymn "A Mighty Fortress Is Our God."

In the latter hymn, pay particular attention to the words "Though this world, with devils filled" (v. 3 in most hymnals). If your class is so inclined have them stand and move to this hymn. Suggest that they shake their fists and stomp their feet. This is an enemy, real and powerful, devious and clever. All our powers of will and wit are needed to do battle with this arch enemy.

Following the singing, emphasize the reality of evil and its power, over and beyond human choosing, and talk about ways it must be fought. Make a list of places and situations where evil is present. Your list may include:

Auschwitz
South Africa
Your hometown
The battle against drugs and organized crime

Experience 66: Evil—Defeat It
(Pre-School and Older)

A third way to teach the understanding of good and evil is by creating a flowering cross. This method is becoming popular in many of our church schools.

The symbol of the rough wooden cross confirms the experience of evil. It illustrates its destructive ways. Yet this same symbol, the cross, points to love, which is powerful enough to conquer evil. Love is the fundamental Christian experience. It is ultimate reality. The power of love is triumphant over evil. That is what all the shouting and glorious music is about at Easter. And, in some mysterious way, for many of us, as Christ defeated evil, he erased the need to explain it.

Directions:
— Bring in a rough wooden cross.
— Cover it with chicken wire.
— Students bring in fresh flowers and stuff the blossoms into the chicken wire. The ugly, rough cross "blooms" and beauty conquers. Love conquers. Good overcomes evil.
— The class shouts triumphantly, "Nothing can separate us from the love of God."

In some churches this flowering cross is created during the Sunday school hour on Easter Sunday morning. Then the cross is carried down the aisle in procession during sanctuary worship. Later it is carried to the front walk of the church and left there to proclaim the Easter message to all passersby.

The closing words of Charles Wesley's hymn, "Love Divine, All Loves Excelling" are "lost in wonder, love, and praise."
May this be our goal in Sunday school. We teach by every means we can, to the end that we and our students come before God "lost in wonder, love, and praise."

OUTLINE OF EXPERIENCES

The following outline is provided as a quick way to identify those experiences that are appropriate for the age group you are teaching. A quick glance will help you find quiet or active experiences, indoor or outdoor experiences, and experiences for large or small groups.

Experience	Page	Large group	Small group	Individual	Active	Quiet	Pre-School	Elementary	Youth Adult	Out-doors	Need Supplies
1.	18		x			x	x				x
2.	19		x			x	x				x
3.	19		x		x		x				
4.	21	x			x		x				
5.	22		x		x		x				
6.	23	x	x		x		x	x			
7.	24	x	x			x		x	x		
8.	25	x	x			x		x	x		
9.	26	x	x			x			x		
10.	27	x				x		x	x		
11.	28	x	x			x			x		

Experience	Page	Large group	Small group	Individual	Active	Quiet	Pre-School	Elementary	Youth Adult	Out-doors	Need Supplies
12.	29	x	x			x		x	x		
13.	29	x	x			x		x	x		
14.	30	x			x		x	x	x	x	x
15.	32	x	x		x		x		x	x	x
16.	34	x			x				x		
17.	42	x			x		x				
18.	42		x		x		x				
19.	43		x			x	x				x
20.	43	x	x		x		x				
21.	44	x			x			x		x	
22.	45	x			x			x			
23.	45	x			x			x			
24.	46	x	x		x		x		x		x
25.	46		x		x			x			
26.	47		x	x		x		x			
27.	47		x	x		x	x				
28.	48	x	x		x			x	x		x
29.	50	x			x			x	x		x
30.	50	x			x			x	x		x
31.	51	x			x				x		x
32.	51	x			x				x		x
33.	54		x		x		x				
34.	59	x	x		x			x	x		x

Experience	Page	Large group	Small group	Individual	Active	Quiet	Pre-School	Elementary	Youth Adult	Out-doors	Need Supplies
35.	60		x		x			x			x
36.	61	x	x		x			x	x		x
37.	62	x	x					x	x		x
38.	63		x		x				x		x
39.	64	x			x			x	x		
40.	65		x			x		x	x		x
41.	65			x		x			x		x
42.	66		x			x			x		x
43.	67	x			x				x		
44.	68		x		x			x	x		
45.	68			x		x			x		
46.	70		x			x		x			x
47.	71		x			x		x	x		x
48.	71		x		x			x			x
49.	72		x		x			x	x		
50.	73		x	x		x			x		
51.	73		x			x			x		x
52.	74		x		x			x			x
53.	80		x			x		x	x		x
54.	81		x	x	x				x		x
55.	81	x	x			x			x		
56.	81	x			x			x	x		
57.	84		x		x		x				x
58.	84		x		x		x				

Experience	Page	Large group	Small group	Individual	Active	Quiet	Pre-School	Elementary	Youth Adult	Out-doors	Need Supplies
59.	85		x		x		x				x
60.	86		x		x			x		x	x
61.	87		x			x		x	x		x
62.	88	x	x		x			x	x	x	x
63.	88		x	x		x		x	x		x
64.	89	x	x	x		x		x	x		
65.	90	x			x			x	x		x
66.	91	x			x		x	x	x	x	x